Make Your Script Sellable

Make Your Script Sellable

The Art and Business of Screenwriting

CARA J. RUSSELL

Waterside Productions

Printed in the United States of America

First Printing, 2021

ISBN-13: 978-1-951805-68-5 print edition
ISBN-13: 978-1-951805-69-2 ebook edition

Waterside Productions
2055 Oxford Ave
Cardiff, CA 92007
www.waterside.com

Contents

A little about me: (intro and acknowledgements)

Kevin Costner inspired me to want to be a screenwriter. My senior year of high school at Western Reserve Academy, I went to see one of his biggest hit movies in our local theatre in Hudson, Ohio. I was the only person to stay through the entire credits, and that is when it struck me: *I want to write movies.*

I majored in communications at Miami University in Ohio, and wrote my first screenplay as an independent study project. After graduation, I moved to Austin, Texas where my first job was as the Assistant Managing Editor and feature writer for a local magazine, County Line Magazine. In my free time, I volunteered as a script reader for the Heart of Austin Film Festival and attended a panel where Callie Khouri (Thelma and Louise, Nashville) and Christopher McQuarrie (The Unusual Suspects, Mission Impossible Rogue Nation and Fallout) among others were speaking. My desire to write screenplays was rekindled even stronger. I moved back to Ohio for a couple years and taught middle school English as a substitute teacher, all the while reading screenwriting books and writing spec scripts.

I was incredibly naïve, like most new writers are, and I sent my first script out to Hollywood production companies. One extremely kind and generous development executive replied, and took the time out of her busy day to speak on the phone to this young, green, aspiring screenwriter. Meg LeFauve (Inside Out, Captain Marvel), who was then working for Jodie Foster's Egg Production, encouraged me to keep writing. She told me that I had "genuine talent

1

and potential." If it weren't for Meg, I likely would not have made the scary move to Los Angeles to pursue screenwriting. I would have stayed in Ohio and gone into teaching full time. Her words were the assurance I needed to hear that I had a chance to make it as a screenwriter. I was also fortunate to have family who supported my seemingly crazy and impossible dream!

My first job in L.A. was also thanks to Kevin Costner: Bull Durham was one of my favorite movies, which led me to becoming the manager of Men's Varsity baseball team at Miami University. It was that qualification that landed me my first job at FOX Sports as Sports Coordinator and Executive Assistant to Jack Simmons, SVP of Sports Production and Operations. Jack was supportive of my screenwriting dreams from day one. I took night classes at UCLA and earned my Writers Certificate from the UCLA Extension Program. I highly recommend all of their classes which are taught by industry professionals.

The first script that I wrote in college, the one that Meg read and discussed on the phone with me, was called THE BASEBALL GIRL. It was inspired by my years on the baseball team, and by those friendships (it was like having a big group of brothers). I reworked that script, retitled it NO PINK TEA after a Ty Cobb quote, and that ended up being the first script I optioned. That option expired, and as of now, that script (which has been updated again) is still available. FYI for any producers who may be reading this!

While I was working at FOX Sports, I was the Head Mentor for FOX's sponsored school for *The Young Storytellers Foundation, an incredible and amazing volunteer organization founded by Brad Falchuk (Glee, American Horror Story, Gwyneth Paltrow's husband) along with several other high powered industry professionals to foster literacy. Every semester we taught a ten week screenwriting program (meeting one hour each week) to fourth and fifth graders in schools across the city. I led a group of ten students and ten mentors to help the kids write a 5-6 page screenplay that was acted out by professional actors at The BIG Show. YSF classes were the highlight of my work day. One of my volunteer mentors was a wonderful producer and now a good friend with whom I have worked on several other projects including SECRET SUMMER and GROOMZILLA. She brought me a book to adapt, and that movie, HEAVENLY MATCH starring Samaire Armstrong and Brendan Penny premiered on the UP Network in 2014. Another of my group mentors who also became a good friend is a prolific Hallmark and Lifetime screenwriter. In 2017 she produced my Christmas short movie, MY CHRISTMAS GRANDPA starring Vivica A. Fox and Bill Cobbs for Lifetime. She also introduced me to the woman I call my fairy godmother, Amanda Phillips. Amanda was the producer who bought my first spec script that I sold, THE BIG GRAB, also titled CAN'T BUY MY LOVE, starring Adelaide Kane and Ben Hollingsworth. It can currently be seen on Amazon Prime, PixL TV, Hallmark Drama, and UP TV. It was Amanda who brought me into my job working as a creative development executive at MPCA, Motion Picture Corporation of America. She is brilliant with story and I have learned so much from working with her.

https://www.youngstorytellers.com/

Brad Krevoy (Dumb and Dumber, plus over 100 movies and TV series) is the founder and Chairman/CEO of Motion Picture Corporation of America. I am beyond grateful to Brad for all the opportunities he has given me as a writer and as a Creative Development executive at his company. I have had three movies produced (and a few currently in development) by MPCA: A VALENTINE'S MATCH on Hallmark in 2020, THE KNIGHT BEFORE CHRISTMAS, starring Vanessa Hudgens and Josh Whitehouse, produced by MPCA, premiered on Netflix in 2019, and I was an uncredited writer on the third installment of a big Netflix Christmas trilogy. I continue to write and work as a Creative Development executive at MPCA and love helping writers develop their own projects.

The movie business is based on relationships. It is true when they say in Hollywood that it is all about who you know. There are plenty of wonderful, good people who genuinely want to help you achieve your goals. However, knowing the right people, people who are willing to read your script and/or hire you for open writing assignments, doesn't do you an ounce of good unless you know how to write an amazing script. The good news is, everyone in this town is looking for an amazing script, and with streamers changing the game, there has never been a better opportunity for new writers to break into the biz.

Which gets me to this book. I have studied screenwriting for 25 years, and at the time of this writing, in addition to my produced credits and associate producer credits, I have 8-10 feature projects in development with various producers and production companies. And now also working on the other side of the table as a Creative Development executive gives me a unique perspective. I have read and given extensive notes on hundreds of scripts that have been passed on and/ or produced for big streamers and networks. I have worked on the production side of projects from the initial pitch through the shooting draft. I often joke or lament after giving upwards of ten pages of notes on submitted scripts that I feel like I am teaching screenwriting 101 or 201, in which case the basics are there, but the script still needs a lot of work to get into a sellable shape.

That is my purpose for writing this book. I want to share and explain the notes that we give to writers on their submitted scripts to help you identify and solve those issues before you submit your script. My goal is to give you an overall guidebook to screenwriting 101 and to help you get your script into sellable shape before you submit it. You usually only get one shot to have your project read, and you want to do everything you can to make sure your script is in the best possible shape. Take it from someone who has been there, and works in both sides of this wonderful, maddening, exhilarating, creative industry, you can make your screenwriting dreams come true!

Congrats!

If you have written your first screenplay, CONGRATS!!! I can't count the number of people who have told me that they have a great idea for a movie, or that their life would make a great movie. I tell them, *"That's fantastic, you should write it."* They usually frown, knowing they are never going to actually sit down and write it. If you have completed a script, you are already ahead of every single person who has *the best idea ever.* You should be proud of yourself, and I hope you had fun writing it. Get ready because now the hard work begins.

The first mistake that many new writers make (I did it, too) is to assume that your first script is amazing, great, and you are ready to reach out to producers and sell this masterpiece that Hollywood didn't know it had been missing and waiting for all this time.

There are always exceptions, especially in Hollywood (depending on who you know) but the likelihood is that your first script, especially the first draft of your first script, is not going to sell. Not yet. That first script I sold, THE BIG GRAB, I rewrote dozens of times, and was open to constructive criticism. Even after I sold it, I wrote so many more drafts that the final movie apart from the characters names and their "cute meet" barely resembled the initial script.

Screenwriting is a long but rewarding journey. Are you ready to begin?

Story

Stories are at the core of our history and culture. Oral traditions in the forms of epic poems, songs, rhymes, chants, and rhymes were used to pass on information from generation to generation, to instruct and teach, share memories, convey tribal and religious customs, and to provide entertainment.

Homer's epic works, <u>The Illiad</u> and <u>The Odyssey</u> were passed down orally until they were physically recorded in print by scribes. Can you imagine having to memorize those epic poems? Memorizing a 3-5 minute pitch doesn't seem so daunting now, does it? For a more in depth study of Greek tragedy, and the dramatic elements of plot, character, and spectacle, I recommend reading <u>Poetics</u> by Aristotle.

Over time, stories were written down, translated, and distributed around the world. Newspapers, magazines, and radio continued sharing stories, but it was the invention of television and film technology that turned storytelling into a visual medium. No matter which medium is used, the core of stories comes down to sharing the human experience and the full range of human emotions.

<u>Universal themes</u> in storytelling are the themes about how we relate to life itself and to each other. Those themes include:

- Power
- Change
- Structure (Systems and patterns)
- Conflict
- Order (vs. Chaos)
- Relationships

One universal theme that falls under relationships is: *relationships change over time*. Perhaps your story is a love story that shows the evolution of a couple that starts with them in love on their wedding day through their bitter divorce. That same theme could also be applied to a story with a different ending. Perhaps you are writing about a married couple who find their way back together after life pulls them in different directions. No matter what your specific story is, everyone can relate to the universal theme of relationships, and specifically in this case that they change over time. Whether that is for better or for worse in the story you want to tell, is up to you as the writer. Your story will be strongest when it is based on your own personal life experiences. The Academy Award nominated MARRIAGE STORY was written, directed, and produced by Noah Baumbach who was going through his own divorce.

If your theme is about power, specifically the abuse of power, that story could be anything from an evil dictator of country to a boss sexually harassing an employee to a lunch monitor taking fellow students' lunch desserts. Every person can relate in one way or another to someone abusing their power over others. GAME OF THRONES is a continual battle for power with many personalities using and abusing power in different ways.

Or perhaps the theme you are writing about is order, specifically in the military. A FEW GOOD MEN is all about an attack that was issued by a General (Jack Nicholson) and carried out by two Privates. The movie questions who should be held accountable and found guilty based on the order of the chain of command in the Marines. Maybe your story is about the order of society at the high school level or at the college level like REVENGE OF THE NERDS. The nerds have to win the Greek counsel in order to have any power at their university, which is run by the jocks and beautiful people.

Whatever your story is, keep in mind what your <u>universal theme</u> is because that is what all people relate to in movies. It is the reason we go to and watch movies. We want to experience, to feel, to relate, and to be entertained.

Writing

Writers often joke that they do everything except write, but when it comes down to it, all you have is what is on the page. Take the pressure off yourself. Don't judge what you are writing while you are in the creative flow. Get it all out. It is like making cookies. You start by assembling the ingredients, combining them properly, making the dough, and then rolling it all out. That is what you are doing in a first draft, rolling out your story. After it is all rolled out, you can go back with the razor sharp cookie cutters and cut the cookies into the perfect shapes.

Keep in mind, if you are bored writing something, that is going to come across and it will be boring to read. Be passionate about your story and your characters. Remember your first crush? The excitement and fear, the thrill and terror, the ecstatic emotional high. Put that energy into your writing. When you are excited about what you are writing, your words will dance with electricity. Your story will be engaging, energetic, and lively.

Writing is work, hard work. It is a job. But it should also be fun. You get to play in the creative sandbox in your mind. You are sharing your imagination and your imaginary friends with the world. When you are having fun writing, it will come across in your writing.

It is important for writers to **read**. Read books, magazines, and screenplays. There are several websites like Simply Scripts, Drew's Script O'Rama, IMDB, where you can find produced screenplays. I know some writers who solely watch movies and TV shows, and that works for them, but that is like learning to cook by watching the servers carry the prepared dishes to the table at a restaurant. You should certainly watch movies and TV shows because this is a visual medium, but ultimately your job is working with words, and crafting stories from those words. Reading is the best way to become a master of words.

Study words, read words, memorize words. Keep lists of your favorite words. Interrobang is one of my favorites. *Why aren't you reading scripts?* Make lists of words for yourself that you can refer back to when you need them. Screenwriters have many fewer words to use as compared to a novelist to tell an entire story. That is why it is important to use the strongest words possible to <u>convey the emotion, attitude, and as much information as possible</u> behind the action in your script.

Take this sentence comprised of four words:

> Meaghan *walks* past Jim.
> Meaghan *saunters* past Jim.
> Meaghan *staggers* past Jim.

The three examples are the exact same except for the verb which is describing the same action of Meaghan walking past Jim. The first example gives you nothing to go on, but the second and third express a different attitude. They paint a different emotional picture and physical state of being for Meaghan. When you write, you want to always choose the words that convey the strongest feelings and actions.

It is important to be **<u>disciplined</u>** in your writing. If writing is your full time job, set your eight hours a day schedule and stick to it. Some people are sharper in the early morning while others prefer to write at night. Find a place where you can focus and get into your creative space or zone. Some people like to listen to music and have background noise whereas others need strict silence. Whatever works for you is fine, the important thing is that you are writing.

It is said that writing is rewriting. Your job is to write, rewrite, and keep writing and rewriting!

The basics of screenwriting:

It all starts with an idea.

J.K. Rowling had the idea for HARRY POTTER pop into her head as she rode a train to Kings Cross Station in London. Stephenie Meyer had a dream about a human girl arguing with a sparkly vampire with whom she had fallen in love, and that turned into the TWILIGHT franchise. A magazine article about street racing in New York City and an illegal street race in LA led to the idea for THE FAST AND THE FURIOUS. An actual fight inspired FIGHT CLUB.

Ideas can come from anywhere at any time. Your job is to be open to them. Think about your own life experiences, your relationships, your family, your friends, the sports you play, hobbies you enjoy, living or historical figures you admire. Think about the tidbits of conversation you pick up from strangers walking by or sitting at the restaurant table next to you, the newspaper articles you read, headlines you see on Twitter. Truth is stranger than fiction, and most of the stuff you truly can't make up. *Tiger King, anyone?* Ideas are everywhere. They are endless. You want to choose an idea that inspires you and ignites your creativity. You are going to be spending many long hours alone in your head with this idea, so pick one that you genuinely feel excited about.

Keep a journal or book, or notes pages on your phone where you can jot down your ideas, dreams, titles, humorous sayings, conversations that you come across, etc. so that you have them to refer back to when you are ready to sit down and start planning your story.

Everything in Hollywood is cyclical. Write what you are passionate about and don't worry about trying to keep up with the zeitgeist. Apocalypse movies, romantic comedies, super hero movies, vampires, zombies, witches, supernatural, pirate, sports … Everything is cyclical. Write what you love and are passionate about, then when your genre cycles back, you'll be ahead of the game with a great script (hopefully more than one!) ready to send out.

However, you do want to make sure that if you are writing a zombie (other) TV pilot, your show is different enough from the other three or four zombie shows that might be currently airing. Do your research. You always want your idea to feel fresh or new. Even if you are recycling an old idea (and most ideas are recycled ones) make sure to give it a fresh and unique twist that we have not seen before.

Ideas:

1.
2.
3.
4.
5.
6.
7.
8.
9.
10.
11.
12.
13. (It's a lucky number!)

An important note before you begin writing:

Production companies and studio development teams receive hundreds or thousands of submissions – scripts, pitches, loglines – from agents, managers, lawyers, other producers, writers, friends of writers, and others every week. It is extremely important that your script looks professional and is properly formatted so it isn't immediately tossed out without being read.

Most professional screenwriters use script software. Final Draft is standard in the industry, but some people use Movie Magic Screenwriter. You may be able to find free screenwriting software on-line, but if you are serious about pursuing a writing career, it is worth the investment to get Final Draft. (Talk to your accountant, if you declare a screenwriting business on your taxes, you should be able to write it off, along with this book and other professional writing expenses.)

Title:

Now back to your idea. Do you have a title? If not, choose a working title for now, and you can always change it later. Just make sure you don't accidentally turn in a blank title page when you submit your script. That happens more often than you would think.

A good title is important. It creates intrigue and interest in the story. It also attracts actors. Samuel L. Jackson signed on to SNAKES ON A PLANE after hearing the title! And from a marketing standpoint, a catchy title helps to sell your movie.

Let's say that you are an executive and your mandate is to find a family friendly dog movie. You have several submissions that are in your inbox queue to read. You are about to jump on a plane and only have time to download one script. Based on the titles alone, which (fictional) script are you going to choose to read first?

ROCKY'S ROAD TRIP
ADVENTURES WITH CARTER AND LUNA
SPY DOGS
BUDDY UNLEASHED

You are going to choose the one that sounds the most interesting and appealing to you, right? Of course, like everything in the movie business, it is subjective. The script itself matters more than the title, which is likely to change anyway, but you want to give yourself every advantage over the competition. Having a great title that jumps out is one way to do that.

Title page:

Formatting your title page: your title page should look like this: [see example]. You want your **title** centered about 1/3 of the page from the top, bolded and underlined. Centered underneath that **Written by**, and centered underneath that, **Your Name**.

In the bottom left hand corner you can list your rep's name and contact information. Many writers like to list their WGA (Writer's Guild of America) registration number if they have registered their script with the guild. You don't have to be a guild member to register your script. https://www.wgawregistry.org/registration.asp This is a way to protect your screenplay. Another option is to copyright it which you can do at www.copyright.gov/

You don't need to use fancy font or colors on your title page. That screams amateur. Stick to the standard formatting. You also do not need to repeat your title and your name on the first page of your script either. That is what your title page is for.

One other note, don't **cheat your script.** That means don't play with the spacing, the font size, or the margins to make your script fit to a certain page length. The production company will know, and we don't like it because when the script is reformatted in a production draft, the cheated page count, whether too short or too long, will throw everything off.

When you submit a spec script (unless you are asked for it for the production draft) you don't turn in the Final Draft file. Instead, there is an option in Final Draft that allows you to "publish" your script to your desktop in PDF – Portable Document Format – Adobe. Submit the PDF File. (When you get into revisions, you will work in revision mode, which *** asterisks and marks your changes so your executives can see what changes were made. You will also want to submit the revision version in PDF and a clean version without the asterisks.)

It should go without saying, but always spell check your script. Proofread your script more than once, and have one or two readers, family members, or friends also proofread it. We all miss the occasional error here and there, and that is not a big deal. *Take it from a writer, your brain really does start to see what you think should be there rather than what is actually there!* However, there is no excuse for sloppy scripts. That just screams lazy writer.

Another issue and a big pet peeve many executives (including myself) have is poor grammar. No one is judging your ability to diagram a sentence, but if someone is claiming to be a professional writer and they do not know their basic subject/object pronouns (she/he/I/we/they vs. her/him/me/us/them) and homophones (your/you're, there/their/they're, past/passed, who's/ whose), they have lost credibility, and most likely, they have also lost their one chance at getting their script read. Which is a shame because they may have truly had a one in a million idea. There are just too many scripts that need to be read and only so many hours in a day. The odds are that the poorly written script is not the one in a million brilliant idea. Make sure you don't knock your script out of contention by not proofreading it before you submit it!

<u>YOUR TITLE</u>

Written by

Your Name

REP NAME AND CONTACT
WGA REGISTRATION NUMBER
OR COPY RIGHT IF YOU CHOOSE

Genre:

Once you have your idea, the next step is to determine what your genre is. Are you writing a romantic comedy, a sweeping epic, or a psychological thriller?

The main genres are: DRAMA, COMEDY, ROMANTIC COMEDY, ROMANCE, THRILLER, HORROR, ACTION, and ADVENTURE.

Subgenres include: MUSICAL, DARK COMEDY, EPIC, PERIOD PIECE, BIO PIC, HISTORICAL DRAMA, WAR, SCIENCE-FICTION, WAR, WESTERN, POLITICAL, CRIME, NOIR, DISASTER, MARTIAL ARTS, ANIMATION, ANIME, FANTASY, DETECTIVE, FAIRY TALE, SUPER HERO, SLASHER, MELODRAMA, SPY, MOCKUMENTARY, FAMILY, EXPERIMENTAL, SPORTS, LEGAL, HEIST, PSYCHOLOGICAL THRILLER, MILITARY, MAFIA, GANGSTER, TEEN, DOOMSDAY, BUDDY COMEDY, WISH FULFILLMENT, and many, many more.

Often movies are a hybrid of two genres. The most common hybrid became its own main category, the romantic comedy. Action Adventure and Action Comedy are also popular.

A less popular combination, Live Action and Animation, was brilliantly done in WHO FRAMED ROGER RABBIT and ENCHANTED.

COWBOYS & ALIENS took a gamble on mixing two very different genres, westerns and sci-fi, and while the movie grossed (the total money earned not deducting expenses) over 100 million dollars, it was considered a flop because of how expensive the movie was to make.

While mixing genres can sometimes spark a brilliant idea, you need to be careful about which ones you mix or combining too many. If you pitch a Mafia Teen Psychological Thriller Doomsday set in the Wild West for your movie, you will most like get a confused "Huh?"

from your executive, followed by, "We have absolutely no idea how to sell that movie, let alone market it."

Hollywood thinks in boxes. It is a business after all. The bottom line comes down to this:

Who is the audience?
Who is the buyer?
How would you market it?

If you can answer those three questions in your pitch, you will be ahead of the game.

Premise:

The premise is a short statement that tells what your movie is all about. It is the main idea or the foundation behind your story. It is similar to a logline, but differs in that it has more to do with what the story is about in a general way.

A reporter goes undercover as a high school senior for her first professional writing assignment. NEVER BEEN KISSED

An underdog boxer gets the chance of a lifetime when he is randomly picked to fight the reigning World Champion. ROCKY

A teen girl enrolls in school as her twin brother so she can prove herself as a soccer player while pretending to be him. SHE'S THE MAN

All of the surviving members of the Avengers and their allies have to put aside their differences and come together to save and restore the Universe. AVENGERS: END GAME

You want to make sure that your premise holds water. It needs to be strong enough to sustain an entire movie. If your story is about a prince who sneaks into a rival prince's castle under an assumed name to steal battle plans and ends up getting hired as the nanny, you might be asked:

If he's a prince, and a known rival, wouldn't they recognize him immediately? And even if they don't recognize him, wouldn't they do a background check on a stranger who comes into the castle and applies for a job that consists of taking care of a young prince or princess? And then what happens? This is idea is not strong enough –yet! – for an hour and a half movie.

Whatever your premise is, make sure that it is strong enough to carry your entire story.

High-concept:

This is a word you will hear often. Everyone wants a high-concept idea. High in this case means <u>elevated</u>, and this means a strong idea with an easily stated premise with a hook that centers around the plot. It means your idea is easy to explain, and the idea is plot and not character based.

JURASSIC PARK is one example of a high concept movie. Cloned dinosaurs come to life in a park. You can easily explain this, and it matters less who the characters are because we already know what to expect with the plot.

HOT TUB TIME MACHINE is another example. The title says it all. It doesn't matter who the characters are, you know this movie is going to be about time travel, and the device is a hot tub.

BIG is about a twelve year old boy who wishes he was "big," and wakes up as an adult. This was one of Tom Hanks' early hits. The idea about a child wishing to be "big" and being granted that wish is considered high-concept as are most wish fulfillment movies with a strong plot hook.

You won't usually hear anyone say low-concept, though it is a term, but rather you will probably be told that your script is <u>not high concept enough.</u>

Movies that aren't high-concept have more to do with character development. The plot is much more understated and character driven. It is more difficult to pitch or explain a movie about a divorced woman who was popular in high school, and returns to her hometown with her young daughter after her husband, who was her high school sweetheart, cheats on her. She has to find a job, realizes that she's a pretty good photographer, and reconnects with a guy who wasn't popular in high school, but is really hot now, and she finds out that he has always been in love with her. And she starts to fall for him, too. HOPE FLOATS with Sandra Bullock and Harry Connick Jr. is a great movie, and one of my favorites, but you can see how it is much more difficult to describe quickly because it all depends on the characters and not the plot.

We were recently pitched a princess movie about a princess who didn't want to accept her responsibilities so she ran away, lived life as a normal girl under a pseudonym, and fell in love with the boy next door. The reason this particular pitch was passed on is that it wasn't high concept enough. This story depends completely on this particular princess' character, and not the plot.

Compare that to this pitch: A princess and a commoner discover that they look nearly identical and decide to switch places and live each other's lives. That second idea, a modern version of Mark Twain's The Prince and the Pauper, is considered high-concept. The plot is much stronger than the first idea, and it depends less upon the specific characters.

A high concept idea will always be easier to pitch and ultimately to sell, which is your goal.

Logline:

A logline is a one or two sentence summary of your screenplay.
This is what you use to entice someone to read your screenplay.
Execs are busy and don't have time to read everything that lands
in their inbox. A logline is their first line of defense to determine
whether or not your script will get read.

From the exec's point of view, it saves everyone time because a logline tells them right away if a project is right for their company or
mandate. If the logline is for a black comedy and the exec is looking for romantic comedies, they will pass on reading your script.
Often times, you will hear that the production company already has
a similar project in development and they are passing on reading
your script after seeing the logline for that reason.

It is your job as a writer to write an intriguing, compelling logline
that makes an exec want to read your script. It is a skill that takes
practice. Some writers may disagree, but I find adverbs and adjectives are your friends, so use them creatively. It takes time to read a
script and there are only so many hours in a day, so you want to use
every possible tool to your advantage to get your script read.

You want to convey who your protagonist is and what their main
conflict is. You can include their goal, what the obstacles are, and
what the stakes are, which may include a ticking clock. There are no
exact rules other than you want to write something that hooks your
reader, and sounds compelling enough to make someone want to
read your script. A general rule is not to use names in the logline.
You can hint at the ending, but don't give it away.

*To catch a dangerous killer and save a young woman's life, a novice FBI
agent enlists the help of a brilliant but incarcerated cannibalistic murderer.*
SILENCE OF THE LAMBS

A medieval English knight encounters a sorceress who sends him to present day USA where he is befriended by a caring high school science teacher who is disillusioned about love, but assists him with his quest which must be fulfilled by Christmas Eve's end.
THE KNIGHT BEFORE CHRISTMAS

Two mothers conspire to match up their grown children – who have a contemptuous high school history – by having them help plan the town's 25th *annual Valentine's Day festival.*
A VALENTINE'S MATCH

Traveling with her snooty mother and rich fiancé, a British aristocrat meets and falls in love with her soul mate, a poor, third class American artist on board the ill-fated RMS Titanic in 1912.
TITANIC

A down on his luck, small-time boxer from Philadelphia who is all heart gets the chance of a lifetime when he is chosen to fight the reigning heavy-weight champion during the United States Bicentennial.
ROCKY

Choose seven (it's a magical number!) of your favorite movies, and practice writing a logline for them:

1.

2.

3.

4.

5.

6.

7.

Short synopsis:

If your logline is intriguing an executive may want a little more information to help them decide if they want to read your script. In which case, they may ask you for a short synopsis. This should be approximately 5-8 sentences long, about the length of a paragraph. It is a longer version of your logline filling in the broad stokes of your story and more details about your characters. You will want to use your characters' names here. This is a sales pitch for your story so make sure it is lively, reads smoothly, and conveys the overall idea of your story.

1-Pager:

One pagers are just that, a one page summary of your movie. They can be for a spec script you have already written, or they can be a pitch for a movie you want to write. The title and your name go at the top of the page followed by your logline. Skip a line or two, and then give a longer summary of your script. Don't think of this as a book report. Book reports are boring. This is a longer sales pitch for your story. Use active verbs, and avoid the passive tense. Have fun with it. This is where your energy and excitement for your story should shine through. You want to make sure you include the set up, the cute meet (rom com), the first plot point, midpoint, the second plot point, and the resolution.

Proven writers often get hired to write screenplays based on 1 page pitches!

Treatments/Story outlines:

A treatment or a story outline can be anywhere from 3-18 pages depending on your personal writing process. Some writers like to write out the entire movie minus the dialogue while others prefer to expand upon the main points in their 1 pager while adding more scenes and details, and even include some dialogue. It is up to you to discuss ahead of time with your development executive what they expect you to turn in to them.

A treatment or an outline gives your executive an overview of the script you plan to write, and allows them to pinpoint problems or change things before you start writing. It is much easier to change or fix something that isn't working in the outline than it is after you have written your first draft.

An executive should not request a treatment or story outline until <u>after</u> you have a signed deal in place because it is considered a <u>step in your deal</u>. More on this in the business of screenwriting later.

Do not submit more than a 1-2 pager/story treatment if you are pitching a script that you want to sell. Unfortunately, there are executives who will try to get as much free work from a writer as possible. It is easier to stand your ground as an established writer. If you are *WGA or guild then you are protected. Non-guild writers don't have that protection, but do have the freedom to take non-guild writing jobs with non-signatory companies (and there are many), which guild writers are not allowed to accept.

*Writers Guild of America West is headquartered in Los Angeles. The Writers Guild of America East is headquartered in New York City

Membership is determined by earned credits. 12 credits makes you an Associate Member. Fees are $100 per year for three years. After the three years are up, if you have not earned the 24 credits needed for full membership, you have to start over.

According to the WGA, you have a five times better chance of being drafted by a Major League baseball team than of getting into the WGA. So if you are already a guild member, congratulations! It is a huge accomplishment. If you aren't a member yet, just keep writing and you will get there!

https://www.wga.org/

https://www.wgaeast.org/

Beat sheet:

Every writer has their own process for organizing their script before they begin writing. Some people like using notecards or whiteboards, and others like scribbling notes on a giant piece of paper. Whatever your process, <u>you should always know the end of your story before you begin writing</u>.

Some writers rely on writing a beat sheet, and other writers skip them completely. A beat sheet lists out every story beat of your movie. It can be a bullet points, sentences, or paragraphs. The helpful thing about writing out a beat sheet is that it helps you make sure that you don't miss any important beats in your story. If you are writing a spec script then the beat sheet is strictly for your own purposes and process.

If you are hired to write a script based on a pitch, your exec may ask for a beat sheet. Like a treatment or outline, it is easier to catch problems in the beat sheet. It is a lot less work for you to fix issues in the beat sheet than it is after you have written a first draft. You will be asked for either a treatment or a beat sheet, not both.

A beat sheet can be as simple as bullet points for the following main beats, or you can list every single beat in your movie.

- *ACT 1*
- OPENING SCENE:
- CHARACTER INTRODUCTION:
- SET UP:
- CUTE MEET (Rom Com)
- INCITING INCIDENT:
- PLOT POINT 1:

- *ACT 2*
- FIRST SCENE IN THE NEW WORLD:
- CHARACTER ARC EMOTIONAL INNER ISSUE ARISES:
- MIDPOINT:
- CHARACTER ARC EMOTIONAL INNER ISSUE AMPLIFIES:
- PLOT POINT 2:

- *ACT 3*
- RESOLUTION:
- (LESSON):
- DENOUEMENT:

Finding your Voice:

Every writer has their own voice or style of writing. The more you write, the more you will fine-tune the expression of your voice. Don't stress about finding your voice. You already have a voice; it is your spirit and energy shining through your words. Your voice is how you choose to share your experience of the world. Like a snowflake, it is unique and unlike anyone else's. Your script will always be strong and better if you write from your own voice rather than trying to imitate someone else's voice.

It is pretty incredible when you consider that we are all working with the same 26 letters in every single thing that gets written. The words you choose and the order in which they are used are what differentiates an okay writer from a spectacular writer. The combination of words and your individual way of expressing yourself through them is where you will find your voice.

A quick exercise to help you find your voice. Answer these questions in 3-4 sentences each:

✓ How did you get through your first major heart-break?

✓ What did you learn from your most embarrassing moment?

✓ What do you regret not saying or doing when you had the chance?

✓ Who is your favorite person on the planet and why?

- ✓ If you could change one thing about yourself what would it be and why?

- ✓ Where do you see yourself five years from now?

How did you answer the above questions? Did you write with honest, raw emotion? Did you answer sarcastically? Perhaps you wrote with humor and the aim of making someone else or yourself laugh. There are no right or wrong answers. However you are most comfortable with expressing who you are and your view of the world is considered your voice.

It is important to express yourself freely and honestly. Don't judge or shame yourself because your voice is important. Don't judge your writing while you are writing, especially not in your first draft. Mute the critical voice in your mind until later when it is time to analyze and rewrite. Don't let the doubts and fears in your mind interfere or stifle your creativity. Let it flow. Your voice matters!

The script:

An exec can determine by looking at the first page of your script if you understand screenwriting. Here is a quick review of the basics. I have been amazed by how many writers attempt to write a screenplay without knowing these important elements, and submit scripts with these common mistakes.

Slugline:

Slugline is an old journalism word that dates back to when printers set type by hand. It let the editors know when they were at the beginning of a new piece, article, or column. In screenwriting, the slugline is used to let the reader know every time there is a new scene. There are three components to a slugline: Interior (INT.)/Exterior (EXT.) – Location – Time of Day

INT. – NANA'S KITCHEN – NIGHT

EXT. – PLAYGROUND – DAY

Every time you start a new scene, you need a new slugline.
This is essential for production. When they go to break down a script and schedule shooting days and locations, they need to know the number of scenes that are going to be shot in each location, and whether the scenes are going to be filmed inside or outside. The time of day is important because movies are rarely shot in order so the lighting crew must plan how they are going to light the scenes. Scenes that take place in the middle of the day are often shot at night and vice versa.

Most professional writers stick to DAY/NIGHT for the time of day. Green writers often leave off the time of day or are too specific.

Ex. 2:30 PM. You don't need to be that specific unless it is essential to your plot, like a murder mystery.

You want to make sure that your sluglines differentiate your locations and don't confuse them. If you are writing a script with scenes that happen in the same place at different locations, ex. Nana's kitchen and Aunt Ann's kitchen, make sure your slugline specifically identifies each kitchen.

INT. AUNT ANN'S KITCHEN – DAY

INT. NANA'S KITCHEN – NIGHT

If you just write KITCHEN in every slugline, production will think all of the scenes are happening in the same kitchen.

Sluglines are also a good place to track time if you need.

INT. TOY STORE – DECEMBER 23rd – NIGHT

An **establishing slugline**, written as **EST.** is a shot that establishes where you are before you jump into a new scene (with a new slugline). This helps distinguish between days and/or different locations. You only need to include a few establishing shots throughout your script when your days start running into each other. You don't need one before every single scene.

EST. THE SUN RISES OVER NEW YORK CITY

INT. FAMILY ROOM – CHRISTMAS DAY

EST. THE SUN SETS OVER MAIN STREET

EXT. GENERAL STORE – NIGHT

If you have characters who are talking on the phone or Facetiming from different locations, instead of writing a new slugline each time one of them speaks, which gets annoying to read as well as to write, you should use **INTERCUT** instead.

*Note that you should always CAPITALIZE a new character the first time you introduce them, and give their age. For adults you don't need to be precise, early 20s, late 20s is better than saying 27. Unless it is essential to the plot. Ex. The story is about Sebastian's upcoming 30th surprise birthday party.

Make sure when you introduce your characters we know who they are. Don't just write a name and then expect the reader to figure out who they are over the next few pages.

INT. NANA'S KITCHEN – DAY

Nana Facetimes with her young grandson, JAMES, 3.

> NANA
> Are you excited for Christmas?

INTERCUT:

INT. STEWART FAMILY ROOM – DAY

James holds the phone to show Nana the Christmas tree.

> JAMES
> Yes! See our tree?

> NANA
> What a great tree. Look at all those presents!

> JAMES
> There's one for you!

INTERCUT allows you to easily write the conversation, and production knows that the conversation will cut back and forth from two separate locations.

When your conversation ends, that will be clear by the slugline for your next scene. So you don't need to write "end intercut."

A quick note about phone and Facetime calls in movies: keep them short. If you can put your characters in the same place, that is always going to be better. I recently had a script come in that had 5 pages of continuous phone calls. No one wants to watch 5 minutes (one script page generally equals one minute on screen) of someone talking on their phone or split screen conversations. It gets boring very quickly. The first phone call was fine to keep in the script, but the writer would be better off finding a way to put the characters together to reveal the information (the purpose of the phone calls) for the other conversations.

LATER is used as a story time connector to show that it is the same day but some time has passed since the previous scene.

INT. STEWART FAMILY ROOM – DAY - LATER

This tells us that we are in the same location on the same day but later in the day as opposed to the scene taking place on a different day.

If you are writing a thriller, you may need to be more specific:

INT. STEWART FAMILY ROOM – DAY – TWO HOURS LATER

You do not need to use *CONTINUOUS* at the bottom of every single page. It is part of some software programs, but if you have a choice, don't use it.

Scene:

You already know that every new scene starts with a new slug-line. However, you don't need to number your scenes. They will get numbered later in a production draft once your script is in production.

The general rule when you write a scene is to **get into the scene late and get out early.** That means avoiding unnecessary action and dialogue at the beginning of a scene.

For example, if you are writing a scene about a married couple fighting about how they are going to spend a windfall check over lunch at a diner, we don't need to see them come into the diner, greet the hostess, talk about the weather, get shown to their booth, sit down, greet the server, order their drinks, be handed their menus, look at the menu, order, and then start their conversation about the money. You can start the scene with the couple already sitting at the table eating their meal and getting into the argument. That is what we mean by getting into a scene late. Unless it is important that your couple greets the hostess. Perhaps she is wrapped up somehow in this windfall money and it is important to have that interaction, then start your scene with the couple coming in and greeting the hostess since that is a crucial moment in the plot.

As soon as the purpose of your scene has been accomplished, whether it is revealing new information or advancing the plot through a character reveal, end the scene. Take our married couple. If the point of that scene is to reveal new information about the windfall check in their argument (perhaps it might not legally belong to them, or the hostess overhears that this couple has come into big money, and we know she's going to get involved in stealing it later) you want to get out of the scene. Get out early. You don't need to drag the scene on by having them keep talking about other irrelevant things, finish their meal, get the check, pay

Make your Script Sellable

the bill, get their coats, and say good-bye as they walk out of the diner.

Every scene in your script needs to have a purpose. That purpose could be informing a character, advancing the plot, building a relationship, or giving new information. You don't want to be writing scenes just to fill empty page space. When you find yourself in that position, you need to go back and rework your story structure and the plot. This is where beat sheets come in handy.

There is a literary saying attributed to many different sources that says you have to kill/murder your darlings. If the line of dialogue, the joke, the character, whatever it is that you absolutely love, if it doesn't add to your story, as much as you love it, you have to cut it.

Every scene in your script must serve your story.

Pacing:

New writers often have long scenes that drag on way too long. Those scenes slow the pacing of your story. You want your scenes to be quick and lively. If all of your scenes run longer than 2 ½ – 3 pages, you may get the note to tighten specific scenes or the entire script. Tightening means cutting out the extra dialogue and action that slow your scenes down. You want concise scenes that move the story along quickly and keep the reader interested.

If you need to have your characters having a long conversation in a very long scene, one way to make it move faster is to tighten the dialogue. Make sure every line is needed. You can break up the scene by moving your characters. Let them go into the kitchen to get the dessert or more drinks. Or step outside. That gives you a new slugline while the scene continues yet breaks it up on the page.

Another way to break up a long scene is with a sub slugline like ANGLE or ACROSS THE ROOM. Let's say that you are writing a long party scene. You can switch to another character's point of view or location from a different place in the same room:

ANGLE

Keely gulps down her glass of wine then quickly refills it.

ACROSS THE ROOM

Alexandra gives Adam a flirtatious glance.

You can also use POV to shift the scene to a specific character's Point of View.

TRICIA'S POV

Tricia tears up as Natalie accepts her diploma.

You don't need to write out an entirely new slugline because you are in the same scene, but it helps break up the long scene a little bit.

Action:

After you have written your slugline, underneath that, you need to set up the action of the scene. This is where you set up what is going on, and the characters who are present in that scene.

Every time you introduce a NEW CHARACTER, early 30s, be sure to capitalize their name, and put their age. If a new name appears and it isn't capitalized, your reader will likely be confused and look back through the previous scenes to see where they missed the character's introduction. You always want to make sure you give each new character an introduction.

Make your Script Sellable

GIGI suddenly appears and interrupts the conversation.

The reader now has to figure out who Gigi is, how she is connected to the characters she is interrupting, and even how old she is.

As opposed to:
Conner's ex-girlfriend, GIGI, 20s, beautiful yet bitter, suddenly appears and interrupts the conversation.

Those few details make a world of difference when added to the action before Gigi's first line of dialogue.

If a character has a line of dialogue in a scene, the general rule is to make sure they are mentioned in the action so they don't just appear out of nowhere with a line of dialogue. Like you read above, if all of a sudden GIGI has a line of dialogue without any introduction in the action, it will be very confusing. The reader will be asking who she is and where she came from.

Screenplay action is not written like a novel where everything is described at length for all the senses. I have read many scripts submitted by talented novelists who pretty much just copied the words from their books into screenplay software. It doesn't work like that. Screenplays are not written like novels. They are two very different skills.

Green writers often spend too much time describing nonessential details like things in the room or what their characters are wearing. Unless it is important to the plot, like *Cinderella disappears, leaving only her glass slipper behind.* In that case, describing the shoe is important since that is how the prince will identify her later. It is significant to the plot. We don't need to know that Cinderella was wearing a French blue, silk gown hand sewn by mice, beautiful white lace gloves that go up past her elbows, mascara, eyeshadow and just a touch of red lipstick, and a diamond clip around her hair which is twisted up in an elegant ponytail with a few wispy strands hanging down around her ears. Those details are fantastic in a novel, but you don't need or want them in a screenplay. *Decked out/beautifully attired/looking like a Princess for the ball* sums up all of the above details in a screenplay.

If your script gets into production, which is your goal, professional hair and make-up, and wardrobe people will be the ones working on the characters' looks and outfits with the producers. Your job is to focus on telling an amazing, compelling story as concisely as possible.

Location scouts will find the house, the kitchen, the playground, so don't waste your precious action space describing the kitchen appliances or the color of the walls, unless again, it is important to your plot. If the blender is a murder clue then definitely mention it, but you don't need to describe all of the other appliances that are also on the counter.

You can and should describe locations as they relate to your characters. We do need to know if they live in a dilapidated hovel or a luxurious penthouse or a suburban house. Choose your adjectives carefully to create the world you are building. **Be as concise as possible.**

Remember that film is a visual medium, and we don't know the characters' thought process unless it is shown on the screen. New writers will often write things like, "She remembers what her friend had said in their past conversation about her ex-boyfriend, and makes her decision," in the action. The problem is, how does the audience know what she is remembering? We don't. She could be thinking about anything. Unless you are writing with voice-over as your device, you have to find a way a <u>show</u> your characters' inner dialogue. If she is feeling nostalgic about her ex-boyfriend in the scene, one option is to have her pick up an old photo of them from

39

happier times. That visually shows us who she is thinking about, and the expression on her face tells us her feelings. She can smile wistfully, longingly, whatever you choose. Her next action will connect us to her decision. She picks up the phone and calls, or she reaches for her purse and coat… Make sure that everything in your action can be shown on screen.

Another issue we run into all too often with new writers, and even some professional writers, has to do with TRACKING which I'll talk more about later. Everything you write in the action and dialogue must track throughout the script. If you tell us that your character is allergic to cats and forty pages later your character is petting a new love interest's cat and not having any signs of an allergic reaction, then that is considered a tracking problem. And for that matter, if you set up that your character is allergic to cats, you want to pay if off. Otherwise, it is irrelevant to your story, and you can delete that unnecessary detail from your script.

It is worth repeating:
<u>Everything you write in your script needs to inform your characters and the story.</u>

Many execs freely admit that they don't read the action. They skip over it completely and only read the dialogue. That makes it even more important to make sure that your action is concise and pleasing to the eye visually on the paper. If you have a big chunk of text, break it up. I like to keep action blocks to 2-3 sentences, four at the most. Anything longer might get skipped.

<u>Make sure you write your action in active, present tense.</u>
If you are writing an action movie, you will be writing more action than dialogue. In that case—

—Skip lines! Keep things moving!

Let's say you have established in a few sentences that EVERETT and GRAYSON are rival archeologists on a dig. They have just discovered a dinosaur bone that will lead to a huge prize for the one who returns home with it.

If a new character enters the scene at that point, go ahead and skip a line and start a new sentence with their entrance. That helps break up your action, and your new character's entrance doesn't get lost in a bunch of sentences. It will also make it easier on the eyes on the page, and easier for your reader to follow what is happening. The worst thing to do is make your reader have to go back and reread sections or even pages to figure out what is happening in your action. They will likely give up, skip the action and skim the dialogue, and toss your script aside.

On the other end of the spectrum, I've worked with writers who skip a line after every single sentence of action. You don't want to do that either as it can mess up the page count (remember, 1 page equals approximately 1 minute of screen time) and can make your script come in too short. It is also annoying to read, and makes the reader think that you are intentionally cheating the script to make it long enough.

There is as saying, *if it's not on the page, it's not on the screen.* This means that what you do write in the action is extremely important. You need to make sure that everything that is essential to your story is included. It is up to you to decide what that is.

You also want to avoid directing in your action lines. Unless you are the writer/director, leave the specific camera angles and shots (two shot, wide shot, close up, pull back, etc.) to the director. Focus only on telling your story.

POV (point of view) is fine to use when needed.

Characters:

After you have set up the action and who is in the scene, your CHARACTERS will be centered underneath the action and the dialogue underneath the character's name. Skip a line in between characters speaking. A screenwriting program will automatically format this for you.

<u>Naming your characters</u>

If your characters have more than a couple lines of dialogue give them a name. You do not need to name insignificant characters. If you name a character, we expect them to be part of the story. Don't number characters if there is only one of them. One script I read introduced BABY #1 as a character throughout. I kept looking and waiting for a second baby to appear in the story but there wasn't one. Also make sure that your characters' names aren't so close that they are confusing to follow. Keeping characters named MEGAN, MADDIE, and MAGGIE straight is much more difficult than following JEFF, WAYLON, and FREDDIE.

Protagonist: The hero is the main character of your story. Even if your hero is an anti-hero, meaning they lack the traditional characteristics of a hero, they are still the lead character.

Antagonist: You can remember this as A= Adversary, or the person who is actively against your protagonist.

Supporting characters: The characters who support your leads and the overall story, but are not the main characters. Your leads, especially in a romantic comedy, almost always need a friend, parent, co-worker, or other confidant.

One mistake I often see is that green writers will make their supporting characters much more interesting, fun, and quirky than their leads. You want all of your characters to be compelling, but make sure that your leads are not boring and dull in comparison. If you find that your supporting characters' story is much more interesting, then try flipping the story and writing it with your supporting characters as the leads instead.

12 Archetypes:

The Swiss psychiatrist, Carl Jung (1875-1961), known as the creator of the field of analytical psychology, introduced the concept of 12 archetypes for human personalities:

- The Innocent
- Everyman
- Hero
- Outlaw
- Explorer
- Creator
- Ruler
- Magician
- Lover
- Caregiver
- Jester
- Sage

*Joseph Campbell (1904-1987), a great mythologist and storyteller, made this concept popular in The Hero's Journey a book that every screenwriter should read for more in depth information.

* *For more on Joseph Campbell and his work, visit the web site of Joseph Campbell Foundation at JCF.org.*

I also recommend <u>The Writer's Journey, Mythic Structure for Writers</u> by Christopher Vogler.

When it comes to creating characters, some writers like to do a full or partial character sketch exercise. They write out everything they need to know about each character and refer back to it when necessary. This can be helpful if you need to track different characters' likes, dislikes, allergies, or whatever you have set up for them and their backstories. Here are several questions that will help you fill out your character sketch:

CHARACTER SKETCH EXERCISE

Where was your character born?
Where did they grow up and in what socioeconomic background?
What is their family like?
What is their attitude towards their family?
With whom was their first kiss?
With whom was their first real relationship?
How and why did that end?
What scares them?
How would you describe them physically?
    Emotionally?
    Mentally?
    Spiritually?
What are their worst/best traits?
What are their strengths?
What are their weaknesses?
Are they aware of their strengths and weaknesses?
Who are their friends?
Who are their enemies, and how did they become enemies?
Where do they live now?
What is their educational background?
Where do they work?
What are their best memories and experiences?
What are their most traumatic memories and experiences?
What quirks do they have?
What do they want more than anything in the world?
What obstacles do they face in getting what they want?
What has held them back from getting what they want so far?
Why do they want it now?
What are they willing to do to get what they want?
How much are they willing to risk to get what they want?
How do they think their life will change after they get what they want?

common development notes on characters:

It is important that you know your characters' backstories. This is everything that happened to your character before the movie began. If two characters dated in high school and will be meeting at their ten year reunion for the first time since graduation, it is important that you reveal their backstory through dialogue. This makes all the difference in what story the reader and audience are anticipating. Did they date all four years then break-up amicably before going to separate colleges? Or did they go one disastrous date and never speak again? Did she break his heart? Did he cheat on her?

Your characters' backstories inform their characters, and set up the tension and conflict we are expecting. You want to choose a backstory that creates the most dramatic tension and conflict. It is much more compelling to anticipate the reunion of two characters who were deeply in love and had a bad break-up in high school, than those who amicably called it quits after a few dates.

Same voice

A note we often give is that all the characters have the same voice. And that is not good. It means that all your characters sound and feel the same. It doesn't matter who is speaking because it is essentially the same person or voice. Each character needs to be unique and distinct. If you can trade lines of dialogue between your characters then you need to reexamine your characters' voices.

Think about your best friends and family members. Each person has their own likes, dislikes, emotions, style of relating to people, style of interacting with others, vocabulary, and cadence of speech. These are the things that will make your characters unique.

When you create your characters, make sure that they don't sound or feel the same. Character sketches will help you make sure that each character is distinct.

One or two dimensional

Another note we give is that a character is one or two dimensional. That means your character doesn't feel real. They have one or two strong characteristics and that is it. That works for a Disney villain, but not for what you are probably trying to write. You want your characters to be three-dimensional with complex emotions and struggles. Actors are drawn to those type of characters as roles they want to play.

Caricature

Occasionally, we will give the note that a character is too much of a caricature. This means that they are so exaggerated that they are past being believable. A mayor in one script we worked on wanted to win her hometown's competition so badly that she was over the top competitively nasty, mean, and rude to every single person, including her young son. It was too much. She was too much of a caricature. Adding some compassion and emotional depth to her character fixed that problem.

A trick I use when creating characters (and this works in real life, too, when you are trying to understand people) remember that: *Everyone thinks they are right.* Whether they are right or wrong, doesn't matter if they believe they are right. Your job is to figure out why they think they are right. To do this, you need to be able to see your story from every character's POV or point of view.

In this scenario, who is right?

A BOYFRIEND punches a RANDOM DUDE in a bar for hitting on his GIRLFRIEND.

The Boyfriend thinks that he is right: This Random Dude needs to be put in his place and taught a lesson about respect, and thus he deserved to be hit.

The Random Dude thinks he is right: He was only talking and being pleasant to this attractive girl. He didn't know her full situation. He didn't deserve to be punched in the face for being friendly in a social atmosphere.

The Girlfriend thinks that she is right: And depending on how you have constructed this character and the story you are telling, she might be mad at her boyfriend for being jealous, possessive and controlling. Or she might feel grateful to her boyfriend for protecting her from a Random Dude who was making her feel uncomfortable and wouldn't leave. Whatever she thinks and feels, she is going to believe that she is right.

In every scene you write, each character has to have their own voice, their own mental and emotional thought process, and you have to track it throughout your script. If you are writing the above scene, you need to be the boyfriend, the random dude, and the girlfriend all at once, and write their actions and dialogue from each of their points of view. That is how you create compelling, dramatic conflict.

Stereotypes
A stereotype is a generalized belief about particular groups of people. It could be racial, gender, cultural, sexual, or specific groups of people. Beware of writing stereotypes unless you are purposely doing so for comedic purposes. You want to create characters that are much more unique and special than falling back on typical stereotypes.

Likable Protagonist
Your protagonist is the character you need your audience to identify with, cheer on, and want to triumph in the end. If you are writing a rom com, you want your lead characters to be likable, sympathetic,

or have at least one strong redeeming quality. That quality can be generosity: Did your character drop several large money bills into Santa's bucket or stop and give money to a homeless person when he/she walked past? Are they nice to babies, children, elderly people, or animals? Do they love their dog like a child? Are they funny? Audiences love funny people even if they are terrible humans. Are they strong, hard-working or passionately devoted to a cause or to their dream? There are many ways to get the reader invested in your protagonist. Even if your character is an anti-hero, there needs to be something that makes us get behind them and want them to succeed. Everyone loves the underdog like Rocky or Rudy. Sympathetic characters are characters we feel for, like orphans. A child who has lost both parents is always sympathetic. Little Orphan Annie, Oliver Twist, Luke Skywalker, and Harry Potter are a few of the most popular ones. Even Lord Voldemort was an orphan, and it is that sole detail that gives us a pang of sympathy for him.

A professional reader who reads scripts for studios and also teaches screenwriting classes (I took his class many years ago), said that he had passed on SWEET HOME ALABAMA when he read it because he didn't think there was anything likable or redeemable about Melanie, the main character. Yet that movie turned out to be a huge hit for Reese Witherspoon and Josh Lucas. It just goes to show that there are exceptions to everything, and everything is subjective.

As for your antagonist, the bad guy or villain of the movie needs to be as strong as or stronger – in the beginning – than your hero. If your antagonist is weaker, you have lost any sense of tension because we already know that your hero is going to win. That is boring. Understanding why your antagonist thinks they are right, and what they are doing to get what they want – often with no regard for the usual moral codes or laws – is the key to creating a strong, fascinating and compelling antagonist. What your antagonist wants should be strictly at odds and in direct opposition to what your protagonist, your hero wants.

<u>Every character you introduce needs to serve a purpose in your script.</u>

I recently gave notes on a script with where the writer had an ELDERLY MAN in a coffee shop getting coffee. He had a few lines of dialogue then we never saw him again. He had no purpose whatsoever other than someone being in a place and filling space by talking about nothing important to the story. Later in the script, an ELDERLY WOMAN was introduced, she had some lines, and then she, too, disappeared. These are considered filler characters. You want to avoid writing characters that exist only to fill up space.

Depending on the budget of your movie, you will likely be asked to reduce the number of characters who only have a couple lines of dialogue to only one or two characters. It is expensive to hire an actor, so from a production standpoint, make sure you don't have too many characters with only one or two lines of dialogue. All of your characters must serve a purpose. If your character gets into a fight with the Ticker Meter Officer who only has a couple lines, that is fine because that is informing your character's temperament and/or part of the plot. A Hostess who says hello and good-bye can be written as smiling hello and waving good-bye. It is much less expensive to cast an extra than an actor who only has one or two lines of dialogue.

Back to the elderly characters in that script mentioned above. The protagonist in that story was a matchmaker. My note was to have the lead character set up the elderly woman with the elderly man and make a love match. That makes not only a sweet moment for the script, it also fits perfectly with the lead character's purpose and career. Or make it a comedic moment and they are not a match. We have been informed that the lead is clearly very bad at her job and that is part of her problem. Either way, the characters now have a purpose other than just filling up page space, and from them we learn more about our heroine.

Think about your favorite movies:
Who do you identify with and why?

What qualities does that character have that makes you like them or root for them to achieve their goal?

Who are your favorite antagonists and what makes you love to hate them?

Consider some of the all-time best villains like Darth Vader, The Joker, Hans Gruber, Hannibal Lecter, and Lord Voldemort:

What qualities and characteristics they have that make them so good at being bad?

How are they as strong as or stronger than the hero, especially in the beginning?

Combining characters
A note we occasionally give is to combine characters. If your lead has two best friends, unless they each have their own strong personality, characteristics and most importantly, purpose, you may be asked to combine them into one character. That happens quite often when two characters serve a similar function in the story. I believe in the original script for MY BEST FRIEND'S WEDDING, Julia Robert's character had two gay friends who were a couple. They were eventually combined into one character played by Rupert Everett.

If you watch ensemble movies, you will see how each character is not only different but they each serve a different purpose in the movie. THE HANGOVER features four guys on a road trip, and each one of them, Phil (Bradley Cooper), Alan (Zach Galifianakis), Doug (Justin Bartha), and Stu (Ed Helms), are very distinct and unique characters with their own voice, attitude, and way of thinking and reacting. Another example is GOONIES. Mikey (Sean Astin), Chunk (Jeff Cohen), Mouth (Corey Feldman), and Data (Ke Huy Quan) are very different characters with their own specific attributes, purposes, and voices.

Casting your script

Another note we often give is <u>don't cast your script</u>. Unless you are writing a very specific story, you don't know which actors will be offered the role, and you don't want to limit any possibilities. Unless it is essential to the plot, avoid describing your characters with specific physical attributes such as 5'9" and blonde hair with blue eyes that turn green when at the sea shore, or 6'4" with thick wavy brown hair and thick eye lashes framing gorgeous brown eyes. That falls under writing like a novelist. Most actors are attractive anyway, so focus on describing your character's essence instead. An "ambitious, money-obsessed workaholic with no time for his family" tells you much more about a character than "tall, dark, and handsome with a charming smile that lights up every room."

There are absolutely times that a character's physical attributes are essential to the plot. In the movie RUDY, it is important to the plot that Rudy (Sean Astin) is a small guy physically because that is an obstacle to his dream of making the Notre Dame Football team. Or the one-armed man in THE FUGITIVE. That physical attribute is instrumental to the plot and solving the mystery. Every word you use to describe and inform your character needs to relate to their character arc and the overall story. If it is not important, consider if you really even need to include it. Replace it with something that is important.

Strong empowered female characters

The current trend is calling for scripts in all genres with **strong, empowered female characters.** The days of the weak, mild, helpless, passive but beautiful woman waiting to be rescued by a man are long gone. Female leads need to be written as strong, smart and/ or wise, and capable. Their goal or purpose has to be more than just getting the guy or getting married. This doesn't mean that you should cut romance out of the movie. Far from it. It means restructuring the romantic relationship so that an empowered woman falls in love with her equal, a true match.

A strong, empowered female doesn't have to go at it alone, that is what supporting characters are for, but she needs to be part of the resolution. She needs to be active in helping solve the mystery, fix the problem, save the world, whatever it is according to your plot. Princess Leia is the perfect example of a strong, empowered and active, not passive, female character. You may have noticed the trend in the recent Disney princess movies. The princesses are much stronger and empowered and help rescue themselves as compared to the original helpless princesses waiting around to be rescued by a prince.

Active vs passive characters

Another note we often give is **characters are passive.** This is not good. Your characters, especially your leads, need to be **active characters.** This means that your characters need to be the ones driving the plot and making things happen. They don't just sit back while things keep happening to them, and just reacting to the plot happening all around them. There have been movies made with passive leads and those movies are usually the ones that bomb. This doesn't mean your characters don't react to things that happen – reactions are comedic gold – but active characters means that your characters are actively involved in making decisions, taking action, pursuing their goals, and doing things that keep the plot moving forward.

Go on-line and look up movies that have bombed. If you watch them, you will see that the chances are high that the lead was a passive character.

A note to male screenwriters: We find that many men often have trouble writing female characters. This is not to say that men can't write female characters well. This is strictly based on the countless scripts I have read where the women are described by their hotness and their tight clothing and how they walk in their high heels that show off their long legs, and how they strip to take a shower. Every single thing they do or say is sexual, and they are all motivated entirely by sex and/or marriage. Cue eye roll.

If you are writing an 80s style sex comedy, go for it. But if this is how you are writing your female characters, you need to rework your approach. Your female characters need to sound, act, react, and think like real people. They also need to relate to each other through their friendships the way real women do.

Here is one way to go about it: Instead of leading with sexuality, lead with your character's emotions. To do that, you have to understand emotions, and you have to know what your character wants, and why they want it. You need to consider what your character is feeling in every situation. Men often say they wish they understand how women think. The answer is that female thinking is a combination of logic, emotions, and razor sharp intuition.

If you get stuck while writing, ask a female friend or family member how they would react or respond in your scene. You may be surprised by what they say.

I find it extremely interesting that most of the fictional male characters that women love, admire, and/or lust over were created and written by women. Fitzwilliam Darcy, Mr. Knightly (Jane Austen), Atticus Finch (Harper Lee), Rhett Butler (Margaret Mitchell), Mark Darcy (Helen Fielding), Sparkling vampires #TeamEdward and hot werewolves #TeamJacob (Stephenie Meyer), Harry Potter (J.K. Rowling), Christian Grey (E.L, James), Gilbert Blythe (Lucy Maud Montgomery), Almanzo Wilder (Laura Ingalls Wilder), Edward Rochester (Charlotte Bronte), McDreamy and McSteamy (Shonda Rhimes), and Outlander's Jamie Fraser (Diana Gabaldon) to name a few. Two notable exceptions are Jon Snow (George R.R. Martin) and Noah (Nicholas Sparks). If you have any others, please let me know!

Character arcs:

When we talk about character arcs it refers to your character's emotional journey and emotional growth. Characters as a general rule have two problems – one is physical, the exterior goal, and the other is emotional, their interior turmoil, inner flaw or weakness. In order for your hero to accomplish their physical goal – get the girl/guy, win the contest/competition, get the prize, whatever it is – they must work through whatever their internal issue/problem/weakness is first. This is considered their character arc. It is what they "learn" along the way, and it is only because they have learned to overcome this internal flaw or issue that they are able to accomplish their physical goal.

The interior problem must relate directly to their exterior goal. This is the secret to writing a screenplay that works.

If your lead character's goal is to win the heart of the girl-next-door, you may choose for his character's weakness to be something along the lines of being shy/fearful/insecure. He then has to overcome that and learn to become confident in himself. It will be that newfound and hard-earned confidence that allows him to make the big gesture at the end and finally win the girl's heart.

Or maybe he doesn't win the girl he thought he wanted because his new confidence has finally helped him realize she is the wrong girl, and the right girl is his best friend who has always been there for him. You get to choose the plot twists, and the choices your character makes will be determined by how he triumphs over his inner issue.

Ask yourself: What does your character need to learn internally to achieve their external goal? What is your character's biggest flaw? How do they triumph and overcome this flaw? Where do they start and where do they end up? This is your character's arc.

In romantic comedies, both leads often have an arc but it is not always necessary. However, your protagonist almost always has an arc.

Structurally, your character's flaw or issue is usually set up in the beginning. It is amplified in the beginning of Act 2 where the depth or extent of your character's emotional issue shows how this is affecting their ability to achieve their goal. Perhaps your hero has an opportunity to get what they want, but they blow it because of their internal issue.

Before the end of act two, plot point two, that emotional issue is stressed again, even stronger this time. It is because your character has not been able to overcome their inner issue or weakness that they hit the all is lost point at the end of act two or plot point two. This is when it can appear that your protagonist is never going to be able to overcome their issue, and it seems like all hope is lost. This is the point in a rom com where the couple go their separate ways, seemingly for good. (We'll talk more about this later with structure.)

It is in the beginning of Act 3 when your protagonist comes to a realization, the moment it all clicks, they get it. This is where they finally overcome their emotional issue, and now they are strong enough emotionally to be able to take the necessary physical actions to achieve their goal.

The stronger your character's arc and emotional journey, the most compelling your character will be.

There are many cop movies, but it was the characters in Shane Black's LETHAL WEAPON that made this movie one of the best in the genre. Two cops (Mel Gibson and Danny Glover) are newly paired up as team, but they are total opposites, with one of them being a suicidal wildcard after the death of his wife. The emotional dynamics in this story are equally or arguably more compelling than their physical goal of needing to catch dangerous drug dealers.

If your character has nothing to overcome, there really isn't much to root for, and we don't really care. That is one note that you don't ever want to hear from a reader or an executive; *I just didn't care about the character(s).*

Your character's backstory is extremely important in regards to your character's arc. It explains why your character has that particular emotional issue. You don't need to go into the entire history or give all the details. It may be enough to know that your character's mom abandoned the family or died when they were young, and not only is your character now sympathetic, we also understand why they are afraid to get too close to anyone and therefore sabotage all of their romantic relationships. The way to introduce backstory is by sprinkling it in through dialogue. Be careful not to get into heavy exposition where you have your characters speaking long chunks of dialogue explaining everything that happened to them. That will get flagged. One often utilized device for sharing emotional back-stories is having your character talk to a therapist. Just ask Mafia boss Tony Soprano (James Gandolfini)'s therapist Jennifer Melfi (Lorraine Bracco).

Writers who have a basic understanding of psychology will be able to write stronger emotional arcs which create stronger, more complex and more compelling characters.

This applies to your antagonists, too. THE JOKER is essentially a movie about The Joker's backstory. We are being shown what happened to him that made him become the deranged, damaged, evil person that he grew up to be.

You want your audience to care about your characters, and that all comes from their arc. We root for characters to change. We want to see them learn and grow and change and then overcome. Another great example is Shakespeare's THE TAMING OF THE SHREW. The teen movie version of that classic play is TEN THINGS I HATE ABOUT YOU. Kat (Julia Stiles) has a clear emotional journey and growth arc. We see her learn about love and watch as she changes from a cynical, sharp-tongued girl into someone who bravely bares her heart and soul when she reads a poem to the boy she loves, Patrick Verona (Heath Ledger), in class. There is a reason this movie has remained a favorite for so many.

It is important to make sure you **track** your character's growth arc. A script I recently gave notes on set the lead character up as a young girl solely focused on being a straight A student who had never had any friends. Her emotional journey was to learn how to care about other people and make her first real friend. That is a great character arc. The problem came in an early scene when the girl went to a fellow classmate's house to ask her for help. The classmate gladly helped and then the two hung out and talked for a while. This is the action of a friend, so clearly the protagonist already has a friend. The character arc that was initially set up has now been completely negated. Every scene must work and fit in regards to your character's arc.

All too often we read scripts where a backstory is set up for the character's arc but then it is completely disregarded or forgotten as the script moves forward.

<u>You must remember and utilize your characters' backstories.</u>

If your character is gay and their backstory is that they came out to their parents as a teenager and were disowned and lived on the streets for several years, that is going to give you a very different character, and be much more compelling, than if your character came out as a teenager to a loving and supportive family. Every interaction and emotional reaction that we see from this character needs to relate back to their backstory as it is part of their arc. You cannot have the character who was disowned and living on the streets happily talking to a coworker about the surprise sweet sixteenth birthday party that their parents threw for them, or the prep school they attended in later scenes. The character who had a loving and supporting family would not have a legitimate reason to complain about being rejected by their parents in a later scene.

The human psyche is intense and complex. We can relate to feeling hurt, pain, angst, loneliness, fear, insecurity. Take a psych 101 class or do some research. Go to a book store and browse the self-help section. You will find a plethora of emotional issues you can use for your characters' arcs.

Possible character arcs (emotional issues to overcome):

1.
2.
3.
4.
5.
6.
7.

Dialogue:

Underneath your character's name, there is a formatted box in which your dialogue goes. It is written centered down the page. (All action always starts at the left margin.) Long chunks of dialogue are the hallmark of new writers, and should be avoided.

NEW WRITER
(yelling)

– Character
– Parenthetical
– Dialogue

The biggest red flag that screams green writer is when there are long chunks of exposition that go on and on, often in complete sentences, giving tons of information, and it does not sound at all like how real people speak when they are having conversations with other real people. If every single character has a long chunk of dialogue that looks like this all the way down the page, that is an immediate give away that the script is not going to be worth an exec's valuable time to bother reading. Trying reading it out loud and you will hopefully hear how unlike your dialogue is when compared to the movies and TV shows you watch. Your actors should not have a monologue in every single box of dialogue. Unless you are Aaron Sorkin, then all your long chunks of dialogue are absolutely brilliant!

Parenthetical – Relating to or inserted as a parenthesis – (—X—) You want to use parentheticals sparingly. You don't want to tell your actors how to act out every line of dialogue. However, since non-verbal communication (gestures, facial expressions, tone of voice, eye contact or lack thereof, body language, and posture) makes up for around 93%

of all communication, occasionally you will want or need to use a parenthetical to make sure the tone and intent of the dialogue are clear.

PAIGE
(teasing)
You're such an idiot.

The context of the scenes, and the adjectives you use in your action usually convey the emotional storyline, but when a line of dialogue could easily be interpreted in the opposite way of what you intend, then that is when you want to use a parenthetical. Again, use them sparingly. Make sure that they are on a separate line above the dialogue. Don't put action in them either. Action goes on the action lines.

You can also <u>underline</u> or *italicize* a word in dialogue to emphasize a word and add an implied meaning.

GRAYSON
Right, because *you're* the winner.

ERIN
I told you, I work for the <u>FDI</u>. Frogs and Dogs Institute.

It takes practice to concisely tell your story's physical and emotional plot in the action lines while using dialogue to reveal information, inform your character, and advance the plot. This is where your use of verbs, adjectives and adverbs is important.

Actors are trained in how to read scripts, break down scenes, and analyze characters. They look at the tone, the conflict in the scene, the character's objective, the words spoken and the emotional beats in that dialogue. They analyze the subtext, how the character feels about everyone else in the scene, the character's perspective on what is happening, and much more. Every single word you use or have your character speak informs their interpretation of that character.

Movie dialogue differs from how people speak in real life. The best way to get an ear for movie dialogue is to watch your favorite movies with the subtitles on. You can see the written words of dialogue on the screen as they are being spoken. It is much more concise than you might have realized.

One exception is family friendly streamer romance and Christmas movies. I'll talk more about those later because they are have their own structure. You can disregard many of the rules you have been taught about writing dialogue when it comes to these types of movies. Characters in these movies speak more like people in real life. Dialogue is more informal, conversational, and uses more filler words.

Honestly, there's nothing really that wrong with filler words, you know what I mean? Yeah, I know, I mean, I just wanna say, just so you know, you don't really want to use them all the time because they sorta take up a lot of space, right? And, if I can also say, it's kinda like not always the most concise way to express your characters.

When you write dialogue, you want to make sure that each of your characters sounds distinct. Think about your family, friends, frenemies, even people you can't stand. They each have their own tone, cadence, speaking pattern, and phrases they favor. Here are some examples of genius dialogue that cannot be interchanged with any other character.

"Can you BE any more generic?" – Chandler Bing (Matthew Perry) **FRIENDS**

"Forget about it" – Lefty (Al Pacino) **DONNIE BRASCO**

"My mama always said life was like a box of chocolates." – Forrest Gump (Tom Hanks) **FORREST GUMP**

"I ate his liver with some fava beans and a nice Chianti." – Hannibal Lecter (Anthony Hopkins) **SILENCE OF THE LAMBS**

"Bond, James Bond." – Every James Bond.

"You can't handle the truth!" – Nathan Jessop (Jack Nicholson) A FEW GOOD MEN

"There's no crying in baseball!" – (Tom Hanks) A LEAGUE OF THEIR OWN

"Yo, Adrian!" – Rocky (Sylverster Stallone) – ROCKY

"Nobody puts baby in a corner." – Johnny (Patrick Swayze) DIRTY DANCING

These are just a few of the hundreds of examples of quotable movie lines. A great actor performing great dialogue leads to unforgettable characters. None of the lines of dialogue above could have been spoken by any other characters in those respective movies.

When you look at your dialogue, if it is interchangeable between your characters then you need to go back and work on your dialogue.

Constructing good dialogue is an art form of its own. One of my favorite examples is from PIRATES OF THE CARIBBEAN: THE CURSE OF THE BLACK PEARL (screen story) (screenplay) | Terry Rossio (screen story) (screenplay) | Stuart Beattie (screen story) | Jay Wolpert (screen story).

There is a scene early on where Jack Sparrow (Johnny Depp) is locked in a jail cell. He tries to get the dog to bring him the key to the cell, but the dog takes the key and runs away. Will Turner (Orlando Bloom) shows up and says, "I can get you out of here."

Now, if you were the screenwriter, what line of dialogue would you have given Jack Sparrow in response? This is where brilliant screenwriters are separated from the rest of us.

A green screenwriter might write:

> ### JACK SPARROW
> *Oh, yeah? Well, then you better hurry up and go find the dog that was just here, because the dog just took the key and ran away with it.*

A more intermediate screenwriter might write:

> ### JACK SPARROW
> *Great! Go track the mutt that was just here. It's got the key.*

The movie's brilliant screenwriters (in 6 words, no less):

> ### WILL TURNER
> *I can get you out of here.*

> ### JACK SPARROW
> *How's that? The key's run off.*

Writing great dialogue is hard. Some writers have an ear and a gift for writing brilliant, clever, fun, and funny dialogue. The rest of us have to work at it. Study screenplays written by top screenwriters, and you'll see the difference.

One more note: Do make sure you introduce your characters' name to the audience at least once. But be careful about overusing your characters' names in your dialogue. If you are still unsure, the next time you watch a movie, pay attention to how many times each character's name is mentioned.

Subtext:

You have the text, and then you have the meaning behind the text. That is called subtext. It is what is meant but not necessarily said. Subtext is reading between the lines to find out what emotionally charged feelings are behind the actual words being spoken.

In real life, people rarely say what they mean. If a man asks his wife, *"Are you okay?"* and she replies with, *"I said I'm fine,"* it is imperative to understand the subtext to know what is really going on underneath the words. To do that, you have to examine each character's physical goal and their emotional state in the context of each scene. Understanding subtext means understanding the true feelings that are being expressed behind the actual words being said.

How many of you immediately read "I said I'm fine," as the wife being annoyed, angry, sarcastic, impatient, or anything except fine? That was you instinctively reading between the limes and interpreting the subtext based on your own experiences because there was absolutely zero context given in those two lines of dialogue.

If you were told that the man had just surprised his wife with a rescue dog, does that change your interpretation of her response? To answer that, you would need to know if a dog was something her character strongly desired or was strongly opposed to. You also need to know her husband's intentions in surprising her with the dog: Was he trying to make her happy and she was crying tears of joy, or was he selfishly doing what he wanted, despite knowing that she didn't want a dog for whatever the reason. Perhaps she was afraid of dogs, allergic, they already have a houseful of pets, etc. In a dialogue polish, if you were going to spruce up her line, "I said I'm fine" into something snappier, you need to know the context and what she is feeling, the subtext, to finesse her line of dialogue.

Many times a character will say the exact opposite of what they mean, making the subtext especially imperative to understand. Take the classic rom com favorite, WHEN HARRY MET SALLY. Harry (Billy Crystal) makes his declaration of love to Sally at a New Year's Eve party. She replies, *"You see? That is just like you, Harry. You say things like that, and you make it impossible for me to hate you. And I hate you, Harry. I really hate you."* Her words are literally stating that she hates Harry, but what she really means, the subtext, is she loves him, too.

Subtext can be obvious or it can be extremely subtle. Either way, it is up to you, the writer, to know what your characters are thinking and feeling at every moment, and from that craft the actual words that they speak.

Common development notes on dialogue:

Your characters have the same voice

You don't want to hear that. It means that all your characters speak and sound pretty much the exact same and/or they have the same mindset and attitude. If you have created unique and special characters with individualized backstories, then the dialogue you write for those characters needs to reflect that. A good way to test this is to see if another character can say the same line. If you can easily interchange the dialogue, then you need to examine your characters' voices.

This includes your characters' ethnicities. I gave notes on a script where a young woman went to meet her Italian relatives for the first time, and was introduced to them as Grandma, Aunt, and Uncle. In Italy, they would be introduced as Nonnie, Zia, and Zio.

Another script about World War Two, had the German characters sounding like modern day Americans using current day swear words and slang.

Make sure your characters speak authentically for whom they are, where they are, and the time period in which your story is taking place.

Too on the Nose

You don't want to hear this either. It means that your characters are directly stating exactly what they are thinking. Dialogue is about subtlety and subtext. When people converse in real life, they rarely say exactly what they are thinking or talk directly about what they trying to get from the other person. Especially when they are talking about an emotionally charged subject.

People drop hints, deny truths they aren't ready to face, tell little white or outright lies, manipulate, or talk around what they really want to say. You don't want your dialogue to be cheesy or cringe-worthy. Especially if you are writing a rom com, you want your leads' dialogue to be fun and snappy banter.

Too Many Clichés

Be careful not to overload your dialogue with worn out clichés. A cliché is a saying, phrase or expression that has become so overused that it is considered boring or unoriginal.

Examples of clichés:

- Actions speak louder than words. ...
- The grass is always greener on the other side. ...
- The apple doesn't fall far from the tree. ...
- You can't judge a book by its cover. ...
- You can't please everyone. ...
- What doesn't kill you makes you stronger. ...
- Love is blind. ...
- Ignorance is bliss.
- Read between the lines
- Play your cards right
- It's an uphill battle
- Better safe than sorry
- Bring to the table

Using a cliché here or there in your dialogue is fine. It is almost unavoidable at times, but you don't want to fill your script with them. Be creative and original when you write your dialogue!

Heavy Exposition

Exposition is a comprehensive description and explanation. It is necessary because it allows you to give information about a character, their backstory, or the plot through dialogue. The danger comes when your script is too heavy with exposition. If your characters are constantly explaining what is going on, talking about what happened before, or giving information about a situation, it is called *heavy* because it is too much. A sign that you are writing heavy exposition is if your characters are speaking in long blocks of thick dialogue.

Too often heavy exposition occurs when you are telling instead of showing. Remember, film is a visual medium.

One of the first rules you learn when you start studying screenwriting is **SHOW DON'T TELL**.

I recently gave a note on a script where a character explained to another character how a Security Guard was doing his job and checking the perimeter of the building that these two characters were planning to break into at the time. Instead of telling all of this information in dialogue, it would be better and much more dramatic, visual, and concise to simply cut to a scene showing the Security Guard on duty patrolling the building thus preventing the break in. The following scene would then continue the conversation without having to explain everything we had just seen.

In another script I gave notes on, Character A told Character B all about Character C being a popular travel blogger and photographer, all the awards he had won, and the number of followers he had. Instead of relaying all of that information in a long chunk of dialogue, it would be better for the writer to find a way to show it instead. Perhaps have Character A pull up Character C's website on a computer or smart phone to show Character B all of the blogger's pictures, awards, and number of followers.

Anytime you find yourself explaining something through heavy dialogue, see if you can find a way to show it instead. Always be aware that film is a visual medium. The more you show and the less you tell, the better.

When you use exposition to give the reader information, you have to make sure <u>that it works logically in the context of the characters and the story</u>.

In another script, two girlfriends were discussing the first girl's plan to get her boyfriend to propose. In their dialogue she discusses her boyfriend and gives her BFF details about him. The writer's purpose was obviously to introduce information about the boyfriend to the reader, but in this context of the characters' relationship, the exposition doesn't work. It brings up the questions: Wouldn't her friend have already met her BFF's boyfriend and know these things? Wouldn't she already know what he does for a living, and where he lives? Any information introduced in this scene would need to be information that is new to the best friend, and not the reader.

<u>Talking Heads</u>
Talking heads are characters that chatter away in a scene, but their conversation doesn't advance the plot, inform a character, or reveal new information. These scenes often go on for pages. If you have two fireman hanging out at the fire station and they are talking about their last call, what they had for lunch earlier that day, what they are going to cook for dinner, about the other fireman they like or don't like, about their respective families, about the most recent news... The reader is left wondering, what about any of this conversation is important to the movie? What is the purpose of this scene?

To fix the problem of talking heads, you need to go back and look at your story plot. Every scene needs to have a purpose. What is the purpose of the conversation? What dialogue is meaningful in the scene? What information is given here that leads to the next scene?

Reaching for the Joke at the Expense of Story

This note often comes up when a writer goes for the gag or the joke in a scene at the expense of the character's arc and the emotional story. If you are writing a straight comedy then this won't be a problem because you have already set up your characters in a comedic way. Otherwise, you need be careful that are you aren't sacrificing the integrity of your character's emotional story by having them crack a joke instead of responding authentically to the situation at hand.

If you have set Patrick up as severely alektorophobic (terrified of chickens) and you place him in a scene and a rooster appears, Patrick's reaction should be in line with his phobia rather than cracking a joke. Even if it is the best cockerel joke you have ever written in your life. Having your character crack a joke here would be at the expense of the story you have set up in regards to his severe phobia.

This isn't to say you can't have your characters joking, but make sure it is in line with their emotional journey and not at the expense of it.

Grammar

I beg you, please have your characters use correct grammar. Yes, I understand that you may have written an uneducated character, but most people have completed elementary school and were taught the basic rules of grammar. You have a responsibility as a storyteller to teach as well as to entertain through your stories. When your write with poor grammar, that is what your audience will hear and repeat. Help people, don't hinder them. Make people smarter and better for having watched your movie or TV show. I continue to be appalled at the number of college educated professionals who do not know their basic pronouns:

Subject pronouns: She/He/They/We/Who
Object pronouns: Her/Him/Them/Us/Whom

Mom took <u>us</u> to the store. Mom took <u>Cole and me</u> to the store. Yet, I constantly hear educated professionals say, Mom took Cole and *I* to the store. (Ahhh!) You would never say Mom took *we* to the store. If you would substitute <u>us</u> then the correct pronoun is <u>me</u>. If you would substitute <u>we</u> then the correct pronoun is <u>I</u>.

I am equally appalled by the number of educated individuals who start sentences with him or her instead of he or she.

Her and her sister went to the store. (Nooo!! Cringe!!) <u>She</u> and her sister went to the store.

I know there are many memes about the kind of people who correct grammar, but as one of our interns baldly put it, "You can insult me, but you still sound dumb."

You are a professional writer. Be smart and sound smart.

<u>Too Stiff</u>
If you get the note that your dialogue is too stiff, it means that it doesn't sound natural. Your characters need to sound like real people. Look at what you want your character to convey in that line of dialogue, and then see if you can find a looser, more natural way of saying the same thing.

CO-WORKER
It is late. I need to leave now.
vs.
It's late. Gotta run.

<u>Overwritten</u>
If you have overwritten your script, that means either your dialogue or your action, or both, are too dense. You have written much more than you need in order to convey what you are attempting to express. You don't need to write five or six action lines if you can

express the same idea in two sentences. If it takes your character 15 words to say something, see if you can say the same thing in half that. To fix overwriting, you need to simplify and condense.

Ingenuine to the character

This means that your character's dialogue doesn't match their characteristics. The dialogue is not authentic to that character. A college English professor should not speak like a street thug. A loving father would not suddenly trash talk kids as if he is someone who dislikes all children. You are creating your characters, so make sure everything they say fits with whom they are. A long time nurse would not shriek and faint at the sight of blood. A mechanic would not be clueless when a group of guys are talking about changing a flat tire.

Sounds Dated

You want to make sure your dialogue sounds fresh, not dated. Unless you are writing a period piece set in the 80s, do your research and learn how modern teenagers are speaking. Gen Z does not speak with the same slang that Gen Xers did. Their cultural references are completely different. If you do include cultural references, make sure that they are relevant to the character speaking.

Many times a writer will submit a script that they wrote ten, even twenty years ago. That is not a problem because it can take that long to get a movie made in Hollywood. However, before you submit an older script, do a pass through it first and update the slang, culture references, technology, and situations that have changed or logically no longer work in today's world. Things like beepers, encyclopedias, political figures and celebrities, popular movies, songs, or shows, etc.

A recent script had a teenage character reference, "Who shot JR?" That cliffhanger was from DALLAS, a popular television show in 1980. It was most likely a reference from the writer's own teenage years. Many people will still recall that episode, but it sounds too dated for a modern teenage character. Your characters need to sound fresh, and be grounded in today's world.

Too Edgy/Not Edgy Enough

Edgy is the opposite of round and smooth and safe. A metal table is edgy, and those sharp edges can cut deeply if you are not careful. In a script that means provocative, unconventional, bold, and even offensive dialogue (and action) that often pertains to violence and sexuality. It is neither good nor bad to write an edgy script, it just depends upon your buyer. Obviously, a family friendly channel is not the place to submit your edgy, dark drama or comedy. And conversely, a streamer that exclusively makes edgy movies featuring heavily with violence and sexuality is not the right place for your sweet and inspirational love story.

Repetition

You want to make sure you aren't repeating the same dialogue, the same information, and the same conversations throughout your script. It is important that you don't repeat the same information, conversations, and dialogue. Don't repeat the same information, conversations, and dialogue. When you repeat the same information, conversations, and dialogue over and over again... *UGH* is right!

Talking in circles

This note comes up quite often. Your story needs to move from beginning to end. Everything in your script needs to advance the plot. When your characters talk in circles, they don't make any headway or forward progress. It is like having the same argument over and over but never resolving it and moving on from it. Your characters need to be always growing and pushing the plot forward.

Preachy

You want to avoid having your characters sound preachy. No one likes being lectured. If you are trying to teach a lesson in your story, find a subtle way to do that rather than having your characters preaching at the audience. Showing, not telling, always works best. The Bishop in LES MISERABLES forgives Jean Valjean after the ex-convict steals his silver by gifting the silver to him in front of the cops who would have thrown Jean Valjean back in prison where he arguably belongs. This act of mercy changes Jean Valjean for good. This scene is much more powerful than had the Bishop merely lectured to his congregation about the importance of forgiveness. Showing an act of forgiveness, kindness, or mercy is always going to be stronger and much more powerful than having a character preach about the same topics.

<u>Needs Finessing</u>
If you are asked to finesse a section of dialogue, or the entire script, it means any combination of the above notes. Finesse means you need to go back through and revise the dialogue. It doesn't mean that you need to throw out entire conversations and start from scratch. It means you need to fix what is already there by smoothing out the dialogue overall and making it better and stronger.

In one script we gave notes on, a 10 year old boy spoke like a 50 year old man in most of his scenes. The writer of that script was a man in his 50s, and he obviously wrote the character in his own voice with his own sensibilities and cultural references, rather than making the dialogue sound genuine for a current day ten year old boy. He was asked to finesse that particular character's dialogue throughout the entire script.

Make sure each and every character's dialogue is authentic to that character's age, gender, race, nationality, family dynamics, education, relationship history, traumatic events they have been through, etc. This is when having a character sketch or your character's back-story written out comes in handy.

Voice-over

Voice-over used to be considered a device for lazy writers, but when it is done right, it works extremely well to give your movie a powerful and effective narration. CLUELESS is one of the best examples of that. I have found that voice-over is usually used most successfully in moves that were adapted from books. For example, STAND BY ME, BRIDGET JONES'S DIARY, and ABOUT A BOY. THE SHAWSHANK REDEMPTION is one of the best examples of voice-over done well.

Make sure you aren't using voice-overs as a crutch, or as a way to cheat explaining through action and dialogue what your characters are thinking and feeling.

Dialogue pass:

If you are asked to do a dialogue pass, it means that the story is good, the action is good, but your dialogue can be better. The best way to do this is to go through the script looking at every line from each character's point of view. Make sure that their dialogue is authentic to that specific character. Then see how you can make it better, stronger, snappier, and more fun.

If you have a scene where your character, a born and raised New Yorker, orders a piece of cheese pizza to go, to make that line stronger, perhaps you change "piece of pizza" to "slice." Your character is still ordering pizza, the action hasn't changed, but now you are making his dialogue more authentic to his character since that is how true New Yorkers speak.

The more specifically detailed and less generic your dialogue, the better it will be. That is why mafia movies are so brilliant. The dialogue is extremely specific to the characters. That is also why people are told to write what you know. When you write what you know, it is specific, unique, and accurate. If you grew up doing competitive cheer, you are going are going to write a much more realistic, accurate, and specific movie than someone who doesn't know a cartwheel from a back handspring. On that note, if you are writing for characters whose world you don't know, make sure you do your research so your characters sound authentic and legitimate.

As you go through your script, ask yourself if the dialogue tracks with each character's goal and purpose throughout the script. Then go back and look at each scene, and how your characters are interacting with each other. What is the subtext in each interaction? Is your dialogue accurately reflecting each character's underlying emotional dynamics? Then read through the script a third time and see how it all flows as a whole.

I recommend inviting friends over for a table read. This gives you the opportunity to listen to your script being read aloud. Professional writers have a table read with the actors before a show is taped. The writers listen, take notes, and revise the dialogue afterwards. Hearing your dialogue out loud is a great way to help you pinpoint lines that sound clunky, don't make sense, jokes that don't land, and so on. If you can, record your table read so you can go back through and listen to it again as needed.

Structure:

A screenplay is the blueprint for a movie.

There have been numerous books written about structure. I liken it to building a house. If you don't start with a strong foundation, your house is going to fall down. Walls, floors, roofs, plumbing, electricity, these are all important elements that go into building your house. If you leave any one of them out, or install them wrong, you are going to find yourself having all sorts of problems at the least, and a complete disaster at the most. The same applies to a screenplay. If your story structure isn't solid, your screenplay is going to fall apart. Once you have your house properly built, strong, stable, and solid, then you can decorate it anyway you like!

There are different types of houses just like there are different movie genres. They all follow the same basic structure. You often hear people talking about breaking the rules, but you have to know the rules to break them. An architect needs to know how to keep the foundation solid and sound in order to build an upside down house. It might appear to have broken all the usual rules but if you examine it, the same rules still apply.

Take THE HANGOVER. The beginning of the movie opens with the second plot point at the end of Act 2 where all hope is lost. The guys have been through hell. Phil is on the phone calling Doug's fiancé to tell her that they can't find Doug, and the wedding isn't going to happen. Then the movie takes us back in time, and we start the adventure. When we get to the second plot point the second time around, however, we see Phil getting tackled before saying what we saw him say before, this time because Stu has just figured out where Doug is! The structure is there, it was just rearranged, but everything is solid, and still works. This is an example of knowing the rules in order to break them, yet still creating a solid movie structure and framework.

It doesn't matter what genre you are writing, the basic rules apply. We tell writers to aim for a 105 page screenplay. That way, later in production and in the editing room, there is room to cut. It is always easier to cut extra scenes from a movie then to be left scrambling to fill time because the movie came in too short. The general rule is a minute a page, so 105 pages equals an hour and forty-five minute movie. Though the final movie will probably be a little over an hour and a half. There is no hard and fast rule on how long your movie should be. There are three hour blockbuster hits like TITANIC and AVENGERS: END GAME, whereas the script for FERRIS BUEHLER'S DAY OFF is only 88 pages long. You generally want to aim for 95-110 pages. A drama can be a little longer. If a writer turns in a screenplay that is too short or too long, it is an automatic red flag that they don't know how to write a screenplay.

A television pilot should be around 30 pages for a half hour show, and 60 pages for a one hour show.

For more in depth information about writing television shows, I recommend the book <u>Write to TV, Out of Your Head and onto the Screen</u> by Martie Cook.

<u>The structure is off/ the structure needs work</u>
When we give this note it means the structure isn't there and what is there isn't working. Your script's blueprint is not solid, and because of that, neither is your story. Go back through your script and make sure that your set-up, cute meet (rom com), inciting incident, plot points, and resolution hit at all the right places. Make sure your character arcs hit in the correct places as well, and that your script isn't too long or too short.

Act 1

Act 1 is usually around 30-35 pages. It sets up your world, your characters, their physical and emotional issues/goals/wants/needs/problems, then kicks your specific story off into motion like a bird taking flight.

You have probably heard that you only have the first ten pages to grab your reader. That is true. *"I read the first ten (or twenty) pages. I was pretty bored,"* is not the feedback you want to get. In those first ten pages you need to set up your world, introduce your lead character, and create a compelling beginning that makes the reader want to continue reading to find out what happens next.

Most action movies open with their character in motion, and often in the middle of a chase sequence. This is one way to immediately grab the reader's attention.

For the other genres, you need to make your reader care about your characters. You want to create an emotional connection that has your audience rooting for your protagonist right out of the gate, and carries the reader along for the entire journey.

Character introductions:

How you introduce your characters is important. Just like you want to make a good first impression when you meet someone, you want to introduce your characters in a memorable way that makes a strong impression. You want your audience to care about what happens to your characters.

Jack Sparrow (Johnny Depp) cockily riding into port on a sinking dingy is one of the best character introductions of all time. Our first impression of this pirate tells us that this character isn't a stranger to crazy adventures, and he is going to take us on a fun and wild ride. We are instantly intrigued and enthralled, and we want to know what is going to happen next. We are sticking around to see what happens next.

That is every writer's main goal: to keep your reader scrolling to the next page because they have to find out what happens next!

Willy Wonka in WILLY WONKA AND THE CHOCOLATE FACTORY is another great character introduction. When Willy Wonka (Gene Wilder) first appears, he is hobbling along with a cane like an old man. As he gets closer he suddenly does a tuck and roll and jumps up with a smile. We instantly know that this trickster is going to keep us, and the sweet and innocent Charlie Bucket, on our toes. And he certainly does.

In Season 1, Episode 1 of GREY'S ANATOMY, we meet Meredith Grey as she wakes up on her couch, late for work. There is a handsome, naked man (McDreamy, played by Patrick Dempsey) on the floor with whom she had a one-night stand. They don't remember each other's names, and shake hands as they introduce themselves again. We find out that she is a surgical resident who is late for her first day of work. Very shortly after that, we find out that her one-night stand is a renowned neurosurgeon who is also one of her bosses. We're intrigued. We want to know what is going to happen next between these two characters. After 16 seasons of this show, the audience is still eager to find out what is going to happen next. That is great writing!

Inciting incident:

This is the event that sets your story in motion. Without this particular incident, you would not be telling this particular story with this particular protagonist. As a general rule, you want your inciting incident to happen before page 15.

One of the biggest mistakes I see from novice writers is that they confuse the inciting incident with plot point 1. They fill the first thirty pages with a very long set up. Things happen then more things happen, and then they finally put their story into motion around page thirty. This is not correct story structure. The inciting incident needs to happen much earlier in the first ten to fifteen minutes of your story.

THE HUNGER GAMES – The inciting incident is when Katniss (Jennifer Lawrence) volunteers as tribute. If she hadn't volunteered, we'd be watching an entirely different movie. We also have a strong, active, empowered female hero. We already like her and are rooting for her because she is sacrificing her own life to save her sister. This happens around page 11 of the script.

THE KNIGHT BEFORE CHRISTMAS – The inciting incident is not always the cute meet, though it can be. Brooke (Vanessa Hudgens) and Sir Cole (Josh Whitehouse) bump into each other at the Christmas Castle, but they go their separate ways. It is when she accidentally hits him with her car that this particular story is set in motion. Because Brooke feels guilty, she invites the knight to stay in her guest house until he recovers from his supposed amnesia. Without this incident, we would have an entire differently movie. This happens on page 13.

HARRY POTTER AND THE SORCERER'S STONE – The incident that sets this story in motion is when Hagrid (Robbie Coltrane) arrives on the island and tells Harry (Daniel Radcliffe) that he is a wizard. Without this event, Harry's miserable life with the Dursleys would have continued as usual. This happens around page 14.

There are always exceptions, and if you know the rules of screenplay structure, your inciting incident can come much earlier or later because everything else in your first act has been redesigned to hold up the house!

ROCKY, the 1977 Academy Award winner for Best Picture, Best Original Screenplay (and more), written by Sylvester Stallone, is one of those exceptions. The inciting incident happens around page 35 when Champion Apollo Creed picks Rocky to be his next big fight. The difference is that the set up isn't just wasting time until the story gets to this inciting incident. It sets up Rocky's character as the underdog we love to root for while also frontloading the subplot romance. It was brilliantly done.

Meet Cute:

In romantic comedies, this is the term used to describe the first time your romantic leads meet. It is usually cute, hence the term. (I often call it the cute meet.) You want the first time your leads meet to be memorable. We want to see their tension, the instant like or dislike. This is the moment the flirt first strikes the rock and we see the sparks flying. This is the scene that prepares us for the eventual burning fire we know the story is building up to between these two characters. We want to see how it is going to unfold. We know they are most likely going to end up together, but the fun is in seeing how they come together despite all the obstacles that you, the writer, have already cleverly set up, and are standing in their way.

We often see romantic leads bumping or banging into each other, and/or spilling something on the other. In THE KNIGHT BEFORE CHRISTMAS, Brooke bumps into Sir Cole and spills hot cocoa (which he calls mead and it becomes a <u>runner</u>) on his suit of armor. In NOTTING HILL, William Thacker (Hugh Grant) bangs into Anna Scott (Julia Roberts) the world's biggest movie star, in a London street and spills orange juice all over her. Technically they meet twice, the first time when she is a customer in his book shop, and then several minutes later in the street. It is the second time they meet that is considered the meet cute.

In THE BIG GRAB/CAN'T BUY MY LOVE, I had my leads meet when they get into a fight over a parking space. This was actually based on an argument I had witnessed between two co-workers.

They were screaming at each other from opposite ends of an office hallway about a parking space that he had self-designated for his own, but since it was not technically his, she had parked there. You will often hear that real life is stranger than fiction, and it is true. You can't make some of this up. If you pay attention, you will find inspiration and screenplay material all day long in your everyday life.

Here are a couple more examples for fun meet cutes/cute meets:

SWEET HOME ALABAMA, Melanie (Reese Witherspoon) engaged to another man, shows up at her ex-husband's house in Alabama after not seeing him for many years and demands a divorce. He is completely stunned to see her and drops the heavy tool in his hand.

BRIDGET JONES'S DIARY, Bridget (Renee Zellweger), wearing a hideous outfit her mother picked out for her, is introduced by her mother at her annual turkey curry buffet to the haughty Mark Darcy (Colin Firth) who is wearing a ridiculous reindeer sweater that his mother picked out for him. We can already see that these two characters "match," but it is going to be a long and bumpy ride until they figure it out, and we are happy to be along for the journey.

The cute meet generally needs to happen in the first fifteen pages for a romantic comedy. If the romance is not the *A story then it can come a little later but still in the first act. If your romantic leads don't meet until the second act, that is way too late. One successful exception you might argue is SLEEPLESS IN SEATTLE. The romantic leads don't meet in person until the very end of the movie. However, Annie (Meg Ryan) hears Sam (Tom Hanks) on the radio very early on, and while it is not in person, her connection and infatuation with him is established. This is structurally in line with where the cute meet needs to happen.

A STORY – This is the main story, the first story or plot line that you are telling. This needs to be your main focus, and the story driving the plot. In a romantic comedy, that is the romance. In a thriller, the mystery is the A story.

B STORY – The first subplot. The B story is the second biggest story or plot line in your script. It fits underneath your A story. If you are writing a thriller and the two rival detectives fall in love while solving the mystery, the mystery is the A story, and the romance would be considered the B Story.

C STORY – The second subplot. It is the third story or plot line but less important than the first two, and will most likely have less screen time. If those detectives solving that mystery have a grandmother and grandfather who meet and fall in love, then that would be considered the C Story.

TV Shows, depending on their format, will have A, B, C, and sometimes D story lines.

Plot point 1:

Plot point 1, sometimes called Turning Point 1 or the First Act Break, happens around page 30-35. This is the point when something happens to your protagonist that sends them and your story in a new direction. There is no going back to how things used to be. And it must happen directly to your protagonist. The first act break obviously ends your first act, and often it ends on the protagonist's reaction to seeing their new world or to the new turn of events.

This is the event that launches your script into your second act or the middle of your movie. You can easily figure out what plot point one is in a movie if you fast forward to the 25 minute mark. Watch the next seven to ten minutes and see what big event happens to the protagonist that changes the direction of the story and puts them in a brand new world – physically, mentally, or emotionally.

I had a writing assignment early on to rewrite a rom com script that wasn't working. One of the reasons was that the first plot point as written was the lead character's group of friends having a conversation about her in a separate location and coming up with a plan to cheer her up. Meanwhile, the lead was just moping in her bedroom. That was it. The way to fix that problem was by tightening the long conversation between the friends without giving away their specific plan then showing the surprise as it directly happened to the lead. The first act ended on her shocked reaction to that surprise when it showed up at her door in the form of a handsome man ready to take her on a date. That took the story in a brand new direction, and whether she accepted or declined the date, there was no going back to her previous mental, emotional, and physical state.

BACK TO THE FUTURE – The first act break occurs when Marty McFly (Michael J. Fox) finds himself completely shocked to be back in time, specifically in the year 1955. This happens around the 30 minute mark. The story has taken a completely new and unexpected turn, and there is no going back for Marty now.

HARRY POTTER AND SORCERER'S STONE – The first act break happens when Harry (Daniel Radcliffe) arrives at Hogwarts. He walks into his new home and school. There is no turning back now. This happens around page 36. Hogwarts is the new world he now faces.

Act 2:

The middle of your story. This is where everything except the set up and resolution takes place. It is the longest act. If a script falls apart, it is usually in the second act. You need to make sure you have <u>enough story</u> to make it all the way through act two. This is why outlines and beat sheets help you before you start writing. They help you make sure you have enough story to carry you all the way through to the end. The main beats of your character arc take place during the second act.

Eric Edson's book <u>The Story Solution: 23 Actions All Great Heroes Must Take</u> is one of the best books that breaks down the story and plot beats that need to take place in a script. I took his class at UCLA, and loved it so much that I took it three times. (He taught different material each time.)

Midpoint:

The midpoint is the middle of your script when you are halfway through the second act. Something big has to happen here. In a romantic comedy, this is usually where the couple becomes intimate, emotionally or physically. The plot has climbed to this point. At the top of the mountain you may expect to find a peak, but you often find a plateau. What your characters do when they reach that high plateau is your midpoint sequence. Do they become intimate by physically having sex or emotionally baring their souls to each other? Do we find out that someone we thought was a good guy is really a bad guy, or vice versa? A midpoint reversal or twist. Does someone get killed? After the midpoint sequence/reversal/twist, your story should be moving like a speeding train racing towards the end of act two.

As you race towards plot point two, your character arcs need to become more amplified. After the midpoint, and right before you hit plot point two, there should be a beat or two where the protagonist's inner issue becomes amplified as the stakes become higher. There is a point where if your character had learned their lesson and been able to overcome their issue, they could have avoided hitting the upcoming rock bottom. Your protagonist has a chance, but they just can't do it yet. They can't overcome their weakness, whatever it is, and because of that, they are going to crash and burn, hit rock bottom, and lose everything.

Plot point 2:

Plot point 2 is known as Turning Point Two, the Second Act break, or the All is Lost moment. In a 105 page script, this comes approximately anywhere from the late 70s through the very early 90s page wise. I've read many scripts that mistakenly have this moment happen too early on page 60, and then the next 45 pages are one resolution after another with multiple endings.

When you have properly structured your movie, this is your protagonist's lowest point. All hope is gone. The game is lost. The antagonist has all the power, and the bad guys have won. The romantic relationship breaks up, and one of the characters moves on to a new job, or goes back to their old life, and possibly even an old relationship. This is your protagonist's lowest point. They hit rock bottom here, and they hit it hard. There is no light at the end of the tunnel. Even if your protagonist has won their original goal, things have changed and they have lost everything after all.

HOW TO LOSE A GUY IN TEN DAYS – Andie finds out that Ben was using her to win an account while he finds out that she was using him for a magazine article. Their anger and angst play out in a terrible song performance and culminate in a fight. Their relationship is completely over. They both lose.

ENCHANTED – Giselle (Amy Adams) falls into a deathly coma at the ball after taking a bite of the enchanted apple. Prince Edward (James Marsden)'s kiss doesn't wake her. As the seconds tick down until midnight, it looks like the evil step-mother has won; Robert's heart is breaking as all hope for Giselle to stay alive is gone and the wrong girl is by his side.

LEGALLY BLONDE – Elle (Reese Witherspoon) quits law school in the middle of the big case after her professor hits on her, and her new friend is disgusted with her, thinking that Elle has used her looks and her body to get where she is. Elle is still unable to overcome her inner weakness, the belief that she isn't good enough and only has her beautiful looks going for her. Because she doesn't believe in herself yet, she quits law school. This is her lowest point, and the end of the second act.

Act 3:

After hitting rock bottom, your character rises and overcomes. They have realized or learned what they needed to learn in order to surmount and resolve the situation, whether it is saving the world or getting the girl or guy.

The third act is the shortest of the three acts. There have been movies with only two scenes in the third act. In a romantic comedy you will often see the girl and guy miserably living their separate lives until one of them has the realization that allows them to overcome what until now has been their emotional stumbling block. In an action movie, the hero is renewed and energized with their purpose, and they now find the strength and determination to defeat the antagonist once and for all. (Or for now, if you are planning on a sequel.) Your protagonist knows what they need to do. They know how to fix the problem. And they do!

Resolution:

Your hero has to <u>earn</u> their resolution. A resolution that is too easy, too contrived, or too convenient will feel like a cheat and a letdown to your audience who has been along for the ride this entire time. No one likes investing in a character's journey only to see the character wake up in bed, and you find out that the entire story was all just a dream. You feel cheated. The same holds true for an ending that wasn't earned by your protagonist.

If your story is about a hero whose gambling addiction destroyed his marriage and led to him being in debt to the Mafia, then he needs to earn the resolution by conquering his addiction, paying off his debts, and saving his marriage through his own efforts. If he does none of those things but instead he buys a lottery ticket and wins enough money to pay off his debts, the resolution is a huge let down to the audience. Not only is it too convenient but your protagonist didn't earn it. It is much more satisfying to watch him overcome his addiction and cleverly find a way to repay the mafia while either winning back his wife or doing things right this time with a new love.

Denouement:

Denouement is a French word that means the final part of the play or movie when all matters are explained or resolved. This often refers to the very end of your script that shows the new world for your protagonist now that their situation/problem/goal has been resolved. Often times, a romantic comedy will end on a wedding. It is the final bow on the resolution that ties everything together, and we get a glimpse of what the protagonist's new life looks like.

NOTTING HILL ends with Anna (Julia Roberts) getting married, and then lying on a London park bench, pregnant, while her husband William (Hugh Grant) reads a book beside her.

Sequels are often set up in the denouement. Now that the original problem has been resolved, there is a hint of a new problem or situation that has just arisen for the hero that they are not aware of yet.

Plot:

The plot is the action that drives your story. Unless you are writing an action movie, your characters always drive the plot.

One note you don't want to get from a development executive is that <u>your plot feels thin</u>. This means that don't have enough happening in your story. Your story needs a substantial plot that is filled with conflict, and fun, exciting, dramatic, and unexpected twists and turns. If you had done an outline or a beat sheet, this is a problem that you would have caught much earlier in the writing process.

On the other hand, you don't want your plot to be overly complicated, either. When there is too much going on with too many characters, the story can be all over the place, and it is too confusing to follow what is happening. When that happens, you will be asked to <u>streamline</u> your plot. That means going back and focusing more on the major plot points in your A story, and reducing the thousand other details and things that are happening in your subplots.

If you are asked to <u>elevate </u>your plot, or your script, that is industry speak asking you to make it stronger and better.

Conflict:

Conflict is defined as a struggle, a clash, or an opposition. Without conflict, you don't have a movie.

There are 3 basic types of story conflict:

CHARACTER VS. SELF

CHARACTER VS. PERSON/PEOPLE
This can be against one specific person, a group of people, or society in general. And within society, you have technology which can be counted as a separate (fourth) type of conflict.

CHARACTER VS. NATURE
This can also include supernatural elements

Conflict is what makes drama. You can have stories without any conflict. All you need is a beginning, a middle and end, but it won't be a structured movie.

Common development notes on plot and conflict:

Well-written but dull
You can have a well-written script that is dull. If you get that note, go back and look at the conflict in your scenes. See how you can elevate it, make it better, stronger, and more compelling. Look at your characters. What do they want? What is standing in their way? Either your protagonist isn't passionate enough about their goal, or the obstacles they face aren't big enough or are too easy to overcome.

Aaron Sorkin is a genius. He can take the dullest subject, like a lawsuit about who founded a social media website, and turn it into a compelling, brilliant story. THE SOCIAL NETWORK was nominated for eight Academy Awards and won three, including Best Adapted Screenplay.

No matter what you are writing about, it is your job to make it compelling, and the way to do that is by creating multi-dimensional characters engaging in dramatic conflict.

Slice of life
This is the note you will get if your script reads like a story without any structure. Something happens, then something else happens, then another thing happens, and things keep happening until you get to the end.

An example would be if your character wakes up, takes a shower, gets dressed, picks up coffee on her way to work, arrives at work, things happen at work, she goes to lunch with a friend and talks about things, then goes back to work, and skips the gym to go to a happy hour with other friends where they talk about more things, then goes home, watches some TV, an ex-boyfriend texts, your character calls her best friend to help her interpret the text, and what she should reply, then she gets ready for bed, and goes to sleep then wakes up and starts her next day.

That is called a slice of life because it is a story about life as it happens. It is not structured like a movie.

It is not a note you want to receive, and unfortunately, it is one we give far too often. It means that the writer has written characters that are doing things and talking about things, but nothing really happens. From the above paragraph, do you have any idea what this movie is about? Or what the main character's goals are? We don't either. Because there aren't any. Yet.

If you are intending to tell this type of story, yes, it is a specific type of storytelling, but movies are meant to be dramatic. That means writing about the interesting things that happen, and leaving out the boring things.

If you are given this note, you need to back to the beginning, and ask, who is your character and what do they want? What are the obstacles to them achieving their goals? You need to study screenplay structure and work on dramatically structuring your story.

Logic holes
A majority of the notes we usually end up giving on a script plot have to do with logic.

Everything that happens needs to make sense according to the rules of the world that you have created or set up for your characters.

This is important enough to repeat: You always need a physical or emotional reason for why your characters respond and act the way they do.

I completely understand, believe me, that when you are writing a story, you are responsible for everything! You are creating worlds, characters, relationships, and dialogue. You are making sure things are structured properly, etc. It is a lot. It really is. And in addition to everything else, you need to make sure that every single thing your characters do and say make sense for the story you have created.

An unhappy writer once argued, *"But it's my story, why can't it be whatever I want it to be?"*
Yes, that is true. It is your story, and it can be whatever you want it to be. If your story is just for you, go for it. If you want your script to sell, then everything needs to make sense. You can't have any logic holes.

When you use your creative freedom to invent a world and the rules in that world, then it is up to you to ensure that all of the characters and their words and actions follow those rules.

The general rule is that the audience will give you one suspended belief. Whether it is believing that a girl pretending to be her brother at a boarding school is genuinely passing for him (SHE'S THE MAN), or that aliens exist and are walking around masquerading as humans (MEN IN BLACK), or that time travel is a real phenomenon (X-MEN DAYS OF FUTURE PAST, BILL & TED'S EXCELLENT ADVENTURE, and OUTLANDER among many others).

Logically, of course we know that aliens aren't going around masquerading as people and ripping off their human faces when they are discovered. We know that people aren't traveling in space ships at light speed through hyper space. That is the one suspended belief you are allowed as a screenwriter. Everything else must make sense logically according to the laws of that world.

One script we received had a wealthy Wall Street tycoon, late 30s, living with a sloppy roommate in a rundown apartment. Logically, this man would be very well off, and able to afford his own place, possibly even a penthouse. He would not be sharing a small, shabby space with a random, messy roommate like he was just out of college. The roommate existed for comedic purposes in the script, but logically, it didn't make sense for the character.

In another script, a man inherited money from a wealthy long lost relative after she passed, but other relatives refused to send him the money. In reality, an estate lawyer is in charge of the assets so this beat in the plot didn't work logically. The writer needed to figure out a way for the characters to circumvent the lawyer in order to make the story work.
If a character gets arrested, in reality they have rights. Whether their rights are upheld or ignored, it logically still needs to make sense in the story.

The good news is that you are creating the world and also the rules. Now it is your job to make sure all of your characters follow those rules.

Too convenient

Another note we often give on plot is that something is too convenient. Scenarios can't exist or happen simply for the convenience of the plot. You want your story to be believable within the world you have created. If something is too convenient it means that it has been included with no regards to the context of the scene.

If a Nevada cowboy is surrounded by outlaws, ready to shoot him dead, and a large crocodile appears out of nowhere, and scares away the outlaws, saving the cowboy, that plot beat would be considered too convenient. Not to mention that it doesn't make any sense logically in the context of a western movie set in Nevada. It was something invented by the writer for the sole purpose of saving the cowboy without any connection to the reality of the story. (However, if you had introduced and set up the crocodile earlier in the story then that beat would work, and this would be considered a fun pay off.)

If your protagonist is desperately trying to find her wedding ring that she lost in her office parking lot, and her boss just happens to show up at work that day with a metal detector then that would also be flagged for being too convenient.

Situations and plot beats need to make sense according to the reality of your story, and not appear for the sole reason of being a convenient solution for your character's current obstacle. If you gave your protagonist a very easy way out of a situation, take another look at that solution and make sure that it works and wasn't just a convenient out for your hero.

Too technical

It can be tempting to want to explain everything, especially if you are an expert in a particular field such as a military officer, an engineer, a scientist, a technician, etc. You want to avoid getting bogged down in too many details in your descriptions that it takes away from the story and the characters. If you are over-explaining then you are most likely telling when you should be showing. Keep in mind that the audience is not privy to what is written in the action, they only see what is on the screen. Also make sure that your characters' dialogue is not filled with explaining everything related to that subject instead of dealing with the story at hand.

A mystery thriller that was submitted to us spent too much time explaining in extreme detail how certain electronic devices were made and how they functioned. All of the action time in the script spent explaining this took away from what would have otherwise been a fast-paced and exciting thriller.

Scenes that are too technical also make the pacing of your scenes drag and can even slow your story to a stop.

Stakes:

One way to test if you have written high enough stakes for your characters is by asking the question, <u>SO WHAT?</u>

If the boy doesn't get the girl, *so what?* If your answer is that he is going to miss out on the one true love of his life, and he is going to regret it for the rest of his life, that is much stronger than eh, he can go back to swiping on a dating app and he'll meet someone new. There are much higher stakes on the first relationship working out than on the second one.

If the detective doesn't solve the murder mystery and the killer goes free, *so what?* If your answer is that the protagonist chalks it up to 'you win some, you lose some' and goes back to work on a new case, the stakes are nowhere near as high than if your detective will be fired for not solving the case, and now her life, her partner's and their children's lives are in extreme danger.

You want to establish the stakes early on, and then up the stakes later during the second half of the second act. Perhaps a promotion is on the line in the beginning, but as the story continues, now their entire job is on the line, or a rival co-worker looks to be edging them out to get the promotion. If a terrorist is holding ten hostages, the stakes go way up for the hero if a hostage is killed, and even higher if the terrorist suddenly reveals that one of the hostages is the hero's wife or child.

The higher the stakes, the better your movie will be.

Ticking clock:

One way to keep your audience on the edge of their seats is to have a ticking clock. This technique or device keeps the script moving and gives the plot a sense of urgency. A ticking bomb programmed to go off at a certain time is the most obvious ticking clock. Any sort of deadline gives you a ticking clock. Something must be accomplished or achieved before a certain time, or there will be major consequences.

In BACK TO THE FUTURE Marty McFly (Michael J. Fox) has to get his parents to fall in love then get the DeLorean up to 88 hours per hour and pass under the wire at the exact moment that the lightning strikes the clock tower.

Use the *So what?* test on your ticking clock to determine if the stakes are high enough. So what if Marty doesn't make all those things? If he doesn't get his parents together, he, his brother and his sister will cease to exist, and if he doesn't hit the wire at the right moment, he will be stuck in 1955. Those are some pretty high stakes!

Another example of a ticking clock is the enchanted rose in BEAUTY AND THE BEAST. If the beast doesn't learn to love and be loved in return before the last rose petal falls, he will forever remain a beast. The stakes are incredibly high here, too, not only for the beast, but for all the servants in his castle who will also be cursed to live forever as furniture.

Even if your character isn't saving the world, the stakes need to be high in regard to how their life will be affected.

Set ups and pay offs:

If you set something up early in your script, you generally want to pay it off. Everything in your script needs to matter. Why would you bother setting up that a character has a severe allergy to chocolate if you never mention it again? However, if you set that up, your audience will enjoy the pay off when later they either have a massive reaction (comedy) or their love interest saves them from that same reaction. Either way, you are paying off something that initially might have seemed like an unimportant detail.

If you set up that your character is a brilliant artist, pay it off in the resolution when they help save their best friend's business. Perhaps your character's contribution is painting a wonderful mural. Having that talent set up early makes the resolution that much stronger than if you introduce at the very end of the script that your character is a fantastic artist.

The most famous payoff is Rosebud in CITIZEN CANE as film students can attest.

One of my favorite character payoffs is in LEGALLY BLONDE. Elle (Reese Witherspoon), a supposed ditzy but beautiful blonde who goes to manicurists in place of therapists, ends up cracking a murder case in court by knowing the chemical science behind hair perms.

You have limited space in a screenplay, so use everything you have. If you get stuck in a scene, go back and see what you might have set up earlier that you could use to pay off now. When you use what you have already established, you add satisfying moments to your script.

Montages:

Montages are a way of showing a lot of activity taking place over a certain period of time. They are often set to music. They are also expensive to film, unless they take place in the same location. A general rule is that you want to limit your montages to one, maybe two. If you have three or more montages, you need to go back to your beat sheet and streamline your plot.

Runners:

A runner is something that runs through or reoccurs throughout the script. It could be a character, a joke, or a line of dialogue.

If every time your character steps outside the house, their eccentric neighbor jogs by wearing a different neon colored kit, you literally have a runner as your runner. Bad pun. Your runners don't have to have a pay off, but they can. Sometimes the joke is that they don't pay off. If your hero has just returned home, bloody and battered, after saving the world which has been completely devastated and destroyed, and then … there goes that same eccentric neighbor jogging past like always, completely unaffected by the devastation. In this case, the runner would be adding comic relief to an otherwise emotionally heavy and intense scene.

In Adam Sandler's movie BILLY MADISON, "O'Doyle Rules," the slogan of a big, bullying family, would be considered a runner because it is a running joke throughout the movie. It culminates in the family's station wagon going over a cliff after slipping on a banana peel in the middle of the road.

A runner usually isn't instrumental to the plot, but it enhances the script with a bit of fun, comedy, or mystery.

Technology:

Technology has changed screenwriting plots. Think about how many movies would (unfortunately) not work if they were made in today's world where almost everyone has a cell phone, GPS, internet access, and social media.

DIE HARD – John McClane (Bruce Willis) would have had a cell phone in his pocket and/or a smart watch capable of making an emergency phone call.

PRETTY WOMAN – Edward (Richard Gere) would have GPS and he would not have needed to stop and ask for directions.

GREASE – Sandy (Olivia Newton John) and Danny (John Travolta) would never have lost track of each other; they would have be texting and following each other on social media.

HOME ALONE – Kevin (Macaulay Culkin)'s parents would have tracked him down by his cell phone in less than a minute. They would also have seen everything going on in their house on their home security smart phone app.

SIXTEEN CANDLES – Facebook would have alerted all her friends and family that it was Samantha (Molly Ringwald)'s birthday. No one would have been able to forget her sweet sixteen.

GOONIES – Imagine how much the plot would have changed if they all had smart phones with GPS.

A screenwriter today has the challenge of creatively working around the problems that having modern technology at your characters' fingertips solves all too easily. You now have to think about how to prevent your character from calling the police or finding someone's identity in less than two minutes while sitting in front of a computer using Google images or facial recognition software. You have to find a way to either use or remove the technology from the equation. If the antagonist smashes the hero's cell phone or throws it in a lake, then that is one problem solved. It is an extra beat in a script that was never needed before.

Keeping up with the latest technology requires you to become more creative to create problems for your characters that can't easily be solved even with all of the modern gadgets at hand. Everyone laughs now at a movie when a character pulls out their beeper but at the time that was the newest form of reaching someone instantly.

Technology has also changed how characters communicate in movies. Maybe one day we will be laughing at texting or Facetime calls. Until then, use technology to advantage in your scripts, and don't let it trip up your plots.

Tracking:

"For the want of a nail the shoe was lost,
For the want of a shoe the horse was lost,
For the want of a horse the rider was lost,
For the want of a rider the battle was lost,
For the want of a battle the kingdom was lost,
And all for the want of a horseshoe-nail."

— Benjamin Franklin

Whether you are writing a mystery or a romantic comedy, everything you set up in the action or the dialogue must track throughout the entire script. This is why it is much easier to fix a problem in the outline than in a completed script.

<u>Not tracking your details is one of the biggest problems and mistakes we see in scripts.</u>

Tracking is also why writers can lose their minds when an executive doesn't understand that a simple note to change one thing is far from simple or easy. It requires a pass through the script to change every single other thing that was affected by that one change. Screenplays are likened to tapestries. If you pull one thread, the entire thing can fall apart.

If you are asked to <u>age down</u> your character, it is not just a matter of changing ALISON *(early 50s)* to ALISON *(early 20s)*. It requires a dialogue pass to make sure that every line is now authentic and appropriate for someone in their early 20s as they relate to the world and to other people. It also requires an action pass to make sure that every action comes from the mentality of someone in her early 20s rather than someone in her early 50s. Everything that you had included that referenced Alison's life between her late 20s to her early 50s now has to be reworked to something that happened earlier during her childhood, high school or college.

All too often, writers have their characters chattering away in scenes about this and that, and they don't realize that every line of dialogue has to track. Filler dialogue often causes more problems than it is worth.

If your female lead, Brooke, talks about how much she loved playing Varsity basketball in high school, that tells us that she is athletic, understands the sport of basketball, and how to plan on a team. That is important information that informs Brooke's character in every subsequent scene. Tracking it means that if you have Brooke run into her love interest shooting baskets at the park in a later scene, you can't forget that she was a competitive basketball player. That is crucial information that will inform how she engages with him in this scene. If she ends up joining him on the court, it is not going to work if you write them getting close physically (your purpose in the scene) by having him teaching her how to shoot a jump shot and her behaving like she has never touched a basketball before.

Let's say you decide you want to keep the scene with the love interest teaching Brooke how to shoot the basketball because it is more important for your story to have this moment of physical chemistry between your leads. You go back and change Brooke's earlier dialogue to her talking about how she was captain of the debate team in high school instead. That works for your basketball scene.

That is one problem solved. But now you need to do a pass through your script and track Brooke's dialogue again. You have now established her as someone who can competently and successfully argue her point of view. She will most likely be confident anywhere she is speaking publically. If that changes too many other dynamics, perhaps you will decide that Brooke played the French horn in marching band, instead.

And just a reminder, anything you set up early on, you should try to pay off later.

<u>Tracking every character</u>
This is what separates the professional writers from the novice writers; making sure every single detail tracks for every single character, and those details ultimately serve your story.

There is an old saying that *God is in the details.* It means the details are important, and paying attention to the small things leads to big rewards.

Conversely, it is also said the *devil is in the details,* which means that not paying attention to the smallest of mistakes in the details leads to failure.

<u>Tracking the timeline</u>
It is important to track your timeline in a script.

If you are writing a Christmas movie, the countdown to Christmas needs to be clear. It will be confusing if you start your story on December first, and then all of a sudden it is Christmas Eve.

Scripts can jump time, you don't need to show every single day, but whatever your timeline is, it needs to be clear. If your script is leading up to a big event, festival, party, or holiday, make sure the timeline and the countdown is clear. Let us know that the wedding is two weeks away, five days to go, three days left, the night before, and finally the day of the big event.

An easy way to do that is to establish time in your slugline or add it in through dialogue. Just make sure that it is clear. I have read scripts where a single day went on for so long that it would be physically impossible for that many things to happen in 24 hours. Keep the action and story moving, break up your days as needed, and track the timeline.

Writing for family friendly channels and streamers:

Family friendly romances that air on channels that are devoted to this specific type of programming are an entity unto themselves. These channels have created a strong, successful brand, and a specific model for their movies that works extremely well for them. These family friendly TV movies, especially their Christmas movies, are light romantic comedies with a heartfelt ending. They provide a sweet escape from reality and the tragedies in the world's news. They allow you to feel good for an hour and a half. That is why people love them so much.

They are not as easy to write as people think. If you want to write a romance, seasonal, Valentine's Day, Spring, Wedding, Summer, Fall, Thanksgiving, or Christmas movie, these are the guidelines that we give to our writers to help them:

Structurally, these movies are often written in 9 acts.
ACT ONE through NINE should be centered and bolded at the top of each act page. If you end an act in the middle of a page, start the next act at the top of a new page.

ACT ONE (TWO – NINE)

END ACT ONE (TWO – EIGHT)

Center and bold END ACT ONE (TWO, THREE through EIGHT) at the bottom of the page. At the end of act 9, you can type **THE END** instead of END ACT NINE.

Open on the lead, always a female, in her world.

By page 10, we need to see the love interest in his world.

The cute meet should happen before page 15.

The first act should end between pages 22-24. The last scene in Act One should end on the romantic leads.

Act Two should be between 12-14 pages.

Acts 3-9 should be no less than 8 pages, but keep their page count fairly equal. You don't want one scene to be extremely long while the others are short.

The midpoint is the middle of Act 4.

The end of Act 8 is your all is lost moment. Your romantic leads have broken up. They have gone back to their old job or old life. Or they have moved away to take a new job. Whatever it is, it looks like there is no hope for this couple.

Act 9 is the resolution. You want to avoid having more than one ending. Save the big kiss until the very end. A tag is fine, but for the most part, once the romance is resolved and your leads kiss, the movie is over.

If you outline your script by scenes, you should have approximately 50 scenes.

Contained is word you will hear often. It means that the movie takes place in a few locations. Fewer locations and characters make a movie much easier to shoot, and much less expensive. Avoid montages because they are expensive to film.

In a romance or Christmas movie, the A story is always the romance. You always want to have a cute and fun hook for your story. There can be a subplot but keep it minimal. The focus needs to be on developing the relationship and the romance between the two leads. You want to build the romance slowly. As far as the time line goes, you generally want to give your characters between ten days to two weeks to fall in love. Play up the sweet, romantic beats between the couple when they finally get together.

There is usually one big set piece, whether that is a festival, a fair, a big holiday party or holiday event, or a wedding. These movies tend to be lower budget, so it is important not to write them too big with too many set pieces or characters. Play up the imagery of the season or holiday you are featuring. If you're writing for Christmas, that could mean ice skating, building a snowman, making snow angels, baking Christmas cookies, decorating gingerbread houses, drinking hot cocoa, getting a Christmas tree and decorating it, hanging up stockings, and kissing under the mistletoe. You don't want to be campy with these, but do you want to use them to give your story that joyful, cozy Holiday feeling. Keep it tasteful.

Your character arcs need to be strong and clearly defined. This is extremely important. You want to set up who they are, what they want, what they hope for, and what their dreams and goals are. Make sure that your characters clearly start in one place emotionally and end up in a new and better place having learned what they needed to learn in order to be with their true love and accomplish those goals and dreams, even if they are a little different than what they started out as. The story belongs to your female lead. She needs to be strong and empowered. She should not sacrifice herself or give up her career for a relationship. You want to show how the couple help each other change and grow for the better as they come together.

Dialogue is looser and more relaxed. The dialogue between your romantic leads should be fun and snappy <u>banter</u>. You can forget most of the rules you learned in screenwriting class about how to write dialogue. Conversational dialogue is encouraged. Filler words are not a crime here. Watch a few of these movies with the subtitles on, and you will see the difference.

You want to keep a quick pace with fun banter. Any scene that goes over two and a half pages needs to be tightened.

These movies are family friendly. These are some of the general guidelines:

Your characters should not be drinking alcohol unless they are giving a toast at a wedding or a special event.

Avoid scenes in bars.

Your characters should not be smoking or swearing.

Don't use the name of the Lord in vain.

Avoid harsh name calling as well as all potentially offensive words and situations.

Pets are fine but make sure there is no hint whatsoever of any kind of animal mistreatment. Characters should not live together unless they are married. If the situation calls for them to share a house, make sure the house is clearly divided into separate sections with a room like the kitchen as the only shared space.

Avoid characters getting divorced or cheating on their spouses.

Avoid physically intimate scenes and sexual innuendos and humor. No sex.

No bathroom humor.

Try to avoid giving your characters too many dead relatives, including parents.

Your characters might have a near miss or two on their first kiss, but save the actual kiss for the end of the movie. Wrap up any other plot lines, and then the romance at the very end. The kiss ends the movie.

Avoid characters who are purposefully deceptive. An accidentally mistaken identity is one thing, but a character purposely deceiving everyone by lying isn't going to get your script greenlit for development.

Avoid strong supernatural elements and anything overly dramatic. You need conflict but it will be lighter than a typical romantic comedy.

Avoid heavy and dark conflict. This includes your characters' emotions and reactions. A few tears is okay, but stay away from anyone sobbing or crying.

You still need conflict, you don't want a "script full of happy people" either. It is a fine balance, and once you find it, you can carve out a career writing these sweet, feel good movies.

The one note we almost always give on these scripts is: MORE ROMANCE, MORE CHRISTMAS (OTHER HOLIDAY).

I liken these types of movies to sugar cookies. Everyone loves a good sugar cookie. It is light, and sweet, but not too sweet, and hits the spot when you have a craving. Once you figure out the formula for the dough (structure) you can have fun decorating each individual cookie (cute and fun hook). As a writer, your job isn't to reinvent the recipe, but to find a unique and fun way to shape and then decorate the sugar cookie. The trick is to have fun and be creative with your approach. Focus on setting up your characters, their arcs, and the romance.

If you go on-line, you will see all the movies that have already been made and aired on these family friendly channels. Read through the synopses so you can make sure you aren't repeating a story that has already been done. Even if your plot is similar, "A busy career woman dating the wrong man returns home to her small town for the holidays and meets her ex-boyfriend/new man," the challenge is to come up with a new hook and twist for that story. You want to find a way to make it different enough from the movies that have already been made but still fits the model.

As for titles, you want your title to be cute, fun, and heartwarming. Remember, the title is going to be the first thing that draws someone to your script. Actors are often pitched several scripts at once. They are sent several script titles and loglines, and what appeals to them the strongest is what they are going to request to read. That is why it is important to make sure that your title and your logline stand out!

Writers block:

Writers block happens to the best of writers. It is frustrating, and the more you stress about it, the harder it is to connect back into your creative flow.

When that happens do something to get out of your head. Go outside, go for a walk, work-out, or listen to music. (Don't ask me why, but listening to One Direction or Green Day gets me back into the creative flow every time!) Do something physical and give your mental functions a break.

Sometimes I will pick up a pen and practice writing with my non-dominant hand. When you write with your other hand, it activates both of the brain's hemispheres which changes how the neurons fire. That opens up a new lane of creative thinking.

Another trick if you are blocked while writing is to reverse the action in your script. If you are trying to get your characters to kiss in a scene, and it is just not working, see what happens if you try the opposite action. Have them get into a fight instead. Completely reversing what you are trying to force to happen often opens up a better pathway that still leads to your eventual goal. It is okay to allow your characters to surprise you along the way. Many times you will come up with something even better than you originally planned.

If you get stuck, go back to what you have already written and use what is already in your script. If you set your character up as a nurse who enjoys knitting in his free time, go back to those details and use them to inform the current situation in which you are stuck.

When you think you're finished, you're not:

You finished your first (or even second) draft, congratulations! You are not finished. Writing is rewriting. Put it away for a while, at least a week or two, and then take it out and go through it again with fresh eyes. Give your script to a couple readers who understand screenwriting structure and get their honest and constructive feedback and notes.

Here is a check list of questions to help you when you are ready to go back through your script:

1. Structure
   A. Did you hit all the plot points in the right places?
   B. Is your script the right page length?
   C. Do the first ten pages grab the reader?
   D. Is the resolution earned?

2. Story
   A. Is the story compelling and a page-turner?
   B. Is the tone consistent?

3. Scenes
   A. Does each scene serve a purpose?
   B. Do you have enough conflict?
   C. Are the stakes high enough?
   D. Are scenes quick and lively or do they drag on?

      E. Is your action concisely written?

      F. Are your characters active and not passive?

      G. Do you pay off your set ups?

4. Do a separate script pass for each character looking at the story from their point of view

      A. Is their voice consistent?

      B. Are they compelling and multi-dimensional?

      C. Are their actions and choices logical?

      D. If they have an arc, do they achieve it?

      E. Look at every single line of dialogue. Can it be improved?

      F. Is the subtext clear?

      G. Do their dialogue and actions track?

5. Grammar check

6. Spell check

7. Title page

Coverage:

Executives at production companies and studios are inundated with scripts from writers, agents, managers, friends of friends, contest winners, and more. It is impossible for one executive or even a small team to read every script that is submitted. Instead, scripts are sent out for <u>coverage</u> by professional readers or interns. They are the first ones to read the script. They write a 2-3 page summary, and assess and evaluate your script. The execs read the coverage, and determine from that if they think the script fits their mandate. If the coverage on a script is poor, the script will most likely get a pass, and the executive won't waste their time reading it. If your script gets good coverage, then an executive will read it. That is your goal. You want an executive to read your script!

As a writer, it is infuriating to think that you might have spent countless hours taking screenwriting classes, studying the craft, and working on writing only to have an intern with little to no screenwriting experience or just a couple writing classes worth of knowledge evaluating your story. As an executive, it is impossible to read all of the scripts that come in, and unfortunately, most of them are not good. That is why coverage is so instrumental and helpful.

Reading scripts and writing coverage is also a great way to earn a little extra money if you have the time. Reach out to production companies and ask them if they need script readers or interns. They may ask you to do coverage on a script they know is either good or bad as a test to see if you know what you are doing. Many colleges offer course credit for internships. If you are a writer doing coverage, make sure you can separate your ego out of it so you can fairly evaluate and judge scripts. If you pass on a great script, or recommend a poor one, you will lose your credibility and most likely be out of a job. No one wants to miss out on a great script, or a great idea that can be made into a great script, even if the execution isn't all that great.

This is a standard industry format followed by the instructions for writing coverage:

THIS COVERAGE BROUGHT TO YOU BY: *YOUR NAME*
TITLE:
AUTHOR:
FORM:
PAGES:
GENRE:
TIME/LOC:
SUBMITTED TO:
SUBMITTED BY:
LOGLINE:

(Excellent / Good / Fair / Poor)
STRUCTURE:
CHARACTERIZATION:
DIALOGUE:
STORYLINE:
SETTING:
(Scale 1 – 10)
COMMERCIAL POTENTIAL:
QUALITY OF WRITING:
STRENGTH OF PREMISE:
COMPELLING STORY:
PROJECT RECOMMENDATION: Recommend/Consider/Pass
WRITER RECOMMENDATION: Recommend/Consider/Pass

SYNOPSIS:

COMMENTS:

Instructions for writing coverage:

LENGTH: Coverage should typically be a few pages total: 2-3 page synopsis, 3/4-1 page comments and critique

PRIMARY BUYERS – Which buyers would be interested in this project

SYNOPSIS – Good coverage tells a story. A list of plot points is not good coverage. Paint us a picture. The highlight reel. Coverage should not read like PowerPoint bullet points. It should give a full sense of the story.

COMMENTS – Keep your comments constructive, but have an opinion. Should the executive take the time to read this script? What is strong about this story? What is weak? What has been seen before? Is this premise fresh? Have an opinion. Would you watch this? Be decisive but fair.

Your comments should touch on these key categories:

1). Originality of Premise

2) Character Development & Motivation – Are these characters compelling? Do they grow and evolve?

3) Plot Construction – Are there enough bumps along the way to make you think this would make a good movie?

4) Expense – What portions of this story will be expensive to shoot? Point them out. Are there expensive set pieces: lots of locations, crazy costumes? i.e., 20 superheroes, period gowns, steampunk, stunts, action, VFX/SFX. Please don't

estimate cost. It is helpful to note areas that might be expensive, but we prefer to leave the budgeting to our production execs.

5) Logic & Plot holes – Where are there jumps in logic?

6) Dialogue – Is the dialogue good, bad, realistic, meh?

7) Similar projects/competing projects in the marketplace?

8) Anything else you deem pertinent, i.e., This script is really misogynist or racist, or the 2nd act falls apart, the stakes aren't high enough, there isn't enough conflict between the characters, the villain doesn't show up until page 90, I didn't know what the script was about until page 45, horrible grammar, typos &/or sloppy writing etc.

The business of screenwriting:

Screenwriting is a business. <u>Tentpole movies</u> (movies that are likened to the poles that hold up a tent) keep studios in business. They are expensive to produce but are considered a low risk and guaranteed to bring an overall profit to the studio. STAR WARS, Super hero movies, HARRY POTTER, and LORD OF THE RINGS are examples of tentpole movies.

<u>Blockbusters</u> are movies that yield two or three times their budget in profits, and their investors see a return.

Most movies don't make money, so the tentpole movies and blockbusters keep studios afloat. Action movies do the best around the world. Comedy is much more difficult because not everyone around the globe relates to American humor.

<u>Indie</u> or independent movies are movies that are produced outside of the main studio system. A smaller movie that surprisingly makes more money than anyone expected or projected is considered a breakout hit. DIRTY DANCING, RESERVOIR DOGS, and LITTLE MISS SUNSHINE are a few examples.

In the past few years, the movie business has been changing thanks to <u>streamers,</u> or streaming services, like Netflix, Amazon Prime Video, Apple TV, Disney Plus, Hulu, Peacock, Warner Plus, Quibi, CBS All Access, etc. New streamers are cropping up every day in addition to all of the usual TV and cable channels, and studios. This is good news for writers because it means there is more need for good content than ever before.

Everyone wants projects based on IP or Intellectual Property. If you can get the rights to a novel, especially one that has been on the New York Times Bestseller list (these are magical words), you increase your chances of getting interest in your project. Buyers like guarantees, and a project that comes with a built-in fan base helps guarantee that there will be an audience for that particular movie. Many of the YA or Young Adult movies that get made are based on books: HARRY POTTER (J.K. Rowling), TWILIGHT (Stephenie Meyer), THE HUNGER GAMES (Suzanne Collins), THE FAULT IN OUR STARS (John Green), THE PERKS OF BEING A WALLFLOWER (Stephen Chbosky), and many more. TV series are often based on book series as well. SWEET MAGNOLIAS (Sherryl Woods) and VIRGIN RIVER (Robin Carr) are two TV shows based on their respective book series currently airing on Netflix. There are movies that you may not even realize are based on books, like George Clooney's MEN WHO STARE AT GOATS (Jon Ronson), and Tom Hanks' FORREST GUMP (Winston Groom).

Getting book rights can be expensive. There are numerous books in the public domain where no rights remain, and therefore you are free to use them as your source material. You may have noticed that many movies get made and remade based on these classic books. To name a few: Shakespeare's plays, Frankenstein, Pride and Prejudice, Emma, Sense and Sensibility, A Christmas Carol, Little Women, Peter Pan, Grimm's Fairy Tales, and Fairy Tales of Hans Christian Andersen. (Disney may own their version of these fairy tales, but the original fairy tales are in public domain for anyone to use!) Because these classics are remade so often, the trick is to come up with a new twist on them. CLUELESS and PRIDE + PREJUDICE + ZOMBIES are twists on Jane Austen's Emma and Pride and Prejudice, respectively, while 10 THINGS I HATE ABOUT YOU and SHE'S THE MAN are modern versions of Shakespeare's The Taming of the Shew and Twelfth Night, respectively. You don't always need to reinvent the wheel as a writer, you just have a new and fun way to roll it out.

Some writers have gone the route of writing a novel, self-publishing it, and then writing a screenplay based on their own book.

Another way to garner more interest in your project is to have a great director or in-demand actor attached. This can work against you, however, if your attachments are not well known. You may not want to promise anyone anything in case your buyer has other people they would prefer to work with or cast.

Know your audience, know your buyer:

A note we often give is, "<u>Read it, liked it, but don't think we can sell it.</u>"

Before you submit your script anywhere, do your research and find the companies that are looking for projects in your genre. You want to make sure that your project fits a company's wheelhouse and/or mandate. If you have a gory horror spec, you are wasting your time by submitting it to a channel that specializes exclusively in family friendly romantic comedies. You are more likely to find success with a company that specializes in the same type of movies as what you have written.

Read the trades and follow which companies are optioning, buying and/or producing what types of genres. This will also keep you clued into the current Hollywood zeitgeist. If you see a slew of romantic comedies, end of the world dramas, or sports movies getting snatched up by production companies, studios, and streamers, you know that will most likely be one of the upcoming trends. And if you have a spec in that genre, now is the time to take it out!

Pitching:

Congratulations, your script is ready to go, and you are now ready to start pitching it!

There are books and classes devoted to pitching. Pitching is essentially selling yourself and selling your idea. The <u>elevator pitch</u> describes the amount of time you would have to pitch your project if you found yourself riding in an elevator with a studio head. Whether you are quickly pitching your idea to someone you just met, or you are going into a pitch meeting, you need to be prepared.

Elevator pitch

An elevator pitch is when you can sum up and pitch your idea in less than thirty seconds or under a minute. You want to include the title, genre, logline, and anything that makes it unique. Is it based on a true story or a personal experience? Do you have a certain actor or director attached? If the person is interested (or too polite to say no), they will say, "Sure, I'll take a look at it," or "Send it over." If this happens, make sure to get their contact information so you can follow through on promptly sending your script!

If you have representation, talk to your agent or manager to discuss the best way to follow up. Your rep may want to submit the project for you, but you should still send an email. Make sure you copy your agent or manager on the email, too. If you don't have representation, you can look into finding a lawyer to represent your project. You don't have to have representation to submit your project. Many companies will not accept unsolicited projects for legal reasons, but in this case, your project is not considered unsolicited since an executive requested to see it.

That is why it is important to remind the executive where you met them in your email. Let them know you appreciate this opportunity, and thank them for their time as you acknowledge that you know how busy they are. Make sure all of your information is included in the email along with a list of your credits and/or your writer's bio. If this is your first project, mention something that will you give you credibility. Did you graduate from film school, where did you study screenwriting, have you won any screenwriting contests, etc. And lastly, don't forget to attach the script! Always double check to make sure you have attached your latest draft of the script in PDF.

You want to make it easy for the executive to have all of your information in one quick look at your email. Keep it short and sweet. No one has time to read a tome. We have had writers sent links to their website that required a case sensitive password to finally access their script after scrolling through all of their other projects. Please don't make an exec jump through hoops to read your script. Many of them may not bother. You want to present yourself as professional as possible. The more professional you are, the more credibility you will have as a writer. This should go without saying, but your email should be written in a professional manner with proper grammar and correct spelling.

If you don't hear back, you can follow up within the week by forwarding your email with your script attachment (but remove the *fwd* from the subject line) and politely reiterate that you know how busy the executive is – if they just had a movie come out, congratulate them on it! – and mention again that it was a pleasure meeting them, and that you just want to make sure that they received your script.

If still don't hear back then it is up to you to determine how you want to proceed. You do need to be proactive in this business, but at the same time you don't want to annoy someone so much that they never want to work with you. Executives are extremely busy and get thousands of emails a week. I would recommend waiting three weeks to a month and trying again. Third time is the charm, hopefully!

Sample follow up email: Obviously you will want to tailor your email to fit your conversation and the situation in your own voice.

Dear Mr./Mrs./Ms. Producer,

It was a pleasure meeting you today at [location]. [Your movie] is one of my all-time favorites (and/or reference something you discussed in person).
I know how busy you are, and I really appreciate the opportunity to send you my drama, titled [TITLE], based on my personal experiences as a [professional mermaid/a true story/other].
Please find attached the script along with my writers' bio. My rep is also copied above. *(If applicable)*
Thank you again for your time and consideration. I look forward to [hearing from you/speaking with you again/other] soon.

Best regards,
NAME

FULL NAME
PHONE NUMBER
EMAIL ADDRESS

Please note that this is just one approach. Every working writer in Hollywood has their own story about how they made it, and no two stories are alike. It is up to you to figure out what works best for you as you navigate your way to success.

Pitch meeting

Whether your pitch meeting is in person or on a video call, pitch meetings can be the scariest part of this entire business for writers. We live in our heads with our characters. We command words from our brains down our arms and out our finger tips. When asked to change the flow of neurons to make the right words flow from the brain and out the mouth, while at the same time reading how people in the room are responding to those words, not to mention feeling the pressure of your entire career on the line…it can be terrifying. Some writers are at ease talking in a room, but most writers experience some form of mild nervous anxiety all the way up to sheer panic.

There are two important things to remember:

1. You know your story better than anyone else.

2. Executives want to hear a good story. It is their job to find great stories that can be made into great movies.

The best advice you can get is BE CONFIDENT because you do know your story better than anyone! And BE PREPARED.
Most executives understand that writers aren't actors.

It doesn't hurt to take an improv class to help you get some practice with thinking on your feet. The best tool I learned in an improv class is to respond with, "Yes, and…" rather than, "No, but…" when someone offers you an idea or suggestion. "No, but…" immediately shuts the other person down and negates what they have just offered; whereas, "Yes, and…" makes them feel like their idea has been heard and accepted. It fosters collaboration and positively builds upon an idea rather than negatively stopping it in its tracks. This is a good tool for interpersonal relationships as well.

If your pitch meeting is in person, always accept the water you are offered. This will help if your throat gets dry or you get nervous.

Start by introducing yourself. Share a little about what other projects you might have done, and something that relates directly to the project you are about to pitch. If your script is about surfing, and you were a professional surfer, that information is not only interesting and makes you memorable, it adds to your credibility as being knowledgeable or an expert about your subject. Or maybe you have never surfed a day in your life, but you have passionately followed the sport for years and have done your research thoroughly. Your enthusiasm and passion for your project are just as important as your expertise to convey in the room.

<u>Enthusiasm and passion are two of the most powerful creative forces in life!</u>

If you know ahead of time who you will be meeting with, do your research and see what connections you can find. Perhaps you grew up in the same city, or went to the same school. Maybe you have friends in common on social media. Perhaps a movie they made in the beginning of their career is one of your all-time favorites. The entertainment industry is based on relationships. You want to make a personal connection in addition to pitching your project.

Make sure you do your research on the company the same way you would before going into an interview. This falls under <u>knowing your buyer.</u>

By the time you are in the room, you should have practiced and read through your pitch at home aloud so many times that you know it by heart. You want to be able to speak easily about it. You don't necessarily want to sound like you memorized it nor do you want to read exclusively from note cards or a piece of paper. The best way is to have bullet point notes on a card or paper that you can speak freely from; and since you have been practicing, let it come easily and naturally. You want to sound conversational, not like you are reciting a book report.

Aim for a 5-10 minute pitch. If you go over 5 minutes, read the room. Short and sweet is better than droning on and on, and boring the room to tears. Keep energy in your voice, no monotones. Everyone wants to see your energy and enthusiasm for the project. If you aren't excited about your own story, why should anyone else be?

Introduce your title, the logline (you should memorize your logline), then mention your lead characters and talk a little bit about them. Then jump into the story. You want to cover the main points of your 1-pager, which includes the essential plot points including the ending.

You don't need to be bouncing off the walls, but do be sure to inject energy and confidence into your pitch. You are not only sharing your amazing story, you are also selling yourself. Be your best self in the room. Executives hope to hear a great story so you have that on your side.
Be friendly, be confident, be prepared, and be enthusiastic about your project.

I don't necessarily recommend this, but when I trip over my words (and I often do), I will apologize with a joke, "I promise I'm much better at writing than speaking." That usually gets a laugh and a couple sympathy points. Pitching is hard for most writers, and executives know that. Do the best you can. Your goal is to get to the next step, whether that is getting them to read your script if you are pitching a spec, to hire you to write the script, or maybe even an option.

One important note, make sure you have other projects ready to pitch. You may give the best pitch of your entire life only to hear, "That sounds great, but I don't think it's for us. What else do you have?" Always be prepared to answer, "***What else do you have?***"This is why it is important to have more than one screenplay completed, polished, and ready to go. You may find yourself in a position of pitching every spec you have written until you land on one that interests the executive. You will lose a big chance if your answer is, "Uh, nothing."

Always follow up with a thank you e-mail along with the script if the executive requested it. If you don't hear back, you can e-mail a polite, follow up e-mail a week or two later. Again, you don't want to annoy your executives by checking in with them incessantly, but you do need to be proactive in your career. Executives are busy and it is likely that they still haven't had a change to read your script or they are waiting to read the coverage of your script first. A gentle reminder about your project is sometimes needed.

Hollywood is built on relationships. If it is appropriate, ask executives to coffee or lunch, and establish a relationship. Everyone likes working with their friends or friendly acquaintances. Make sure you get the assistants' names, and network with them as well. One day those assistants could be the show runner, an executive, or running the department. Be polite to everyone. Network and cultivate your relationships.

It is important that you don't put all your screenwriting dreams and hopes into any one submission. Keep writing, keep networking, and keep pitching!

Writing on Spec:

A spec or speculative screenplay means that it is unsolicited. No one asked you or paid you to write it for them. You own your spec scripts one hundred percent. Specs can be sold, optioned, or sent out as a writing sample to get you meetings. If you want to write for TV, your spec could be an original pilot or an episode of an existing show.

An executive should never ask you to write anything for them on spec. However, they can tell you that if you do end up writing your spec script, they would be happy to read it. This is good because it means you have an open door with a production company. They are willing to read your script, and that is your first goal after you write a script. To get it read!

Some reps tell their writers to never write on spec or for free. My advice is to trust your instincts. I've been on both sides of this one. As a writer, I have written several projects on spec for producers. I chose to write for free with an agreement saying that if/when the script sells to a buyer then the contract would be negotiated. My reasons for that were 1) I was going to be writing spec scripts anyway 2) I would have legitimate producers putting in their time to give me notes, and they would later be putting their energy into hopefully selling the script, 3) I was happy to work with high level producers, and 4) I was able to say in meetings and put on my resume that I had a project in development with *So & So* which gave me credibility and opened more doors. Three of those specs are actively being shopped now. For me, it was worth it. Every script you write, makes you a better writer. And I still have those three scripts as viable properties that will hopefully sell and be produced.

Many production companies have limited development funds. If they are going to pay for a script, they are going to go with a produced writer over a new, unproven writer. I often give notes to new writers who are working on spec scripts that just aren't strong enough (that is the industry way of saying they aren't good enough) to be optioned. I want to help these writers get their scripts into a strong enough place so that they can be optioned. That is your goal with a spec script, to get it optioned and/or sold.

Giving Notes:

It is pretty standard to use the Oreo technique when you are giving a writer notes. Start with a positive, give the notes, and end on a positive. If you are asked to give notes on a friend's script, you can use the coverage guidelines to help you present your comments. This isn't about not hurting someone's feelings or bruising their ego, it is about giving constructive notes to help get a script into sellable shape. That is the goal.

In a notes meeting, "Let me <u>pitch</u> you this idea ..." or "I'm going to <u>pitch</u> this idea ..." is industry speak for *here are my ideas and suggestions.*

Taking Notes:

Accept the notes. Being on both sides of the table, I have found that it is always helpful to get a fresh perspective from a new set of eyes. As a writer, most of the notes I have been given by executives have only helped make my script that much better and gotten it a greenlight and into production. That is your end goal. I am always appreciative that someone took the time (and everyone's time is valuable) to read my script, write down notes, and then share those notes with me to make my script better.

If there are notes I don't agree with, and it happens, I take them anyway, and I can discuss them later during the rewrite. Creative execs who understand story are open to talking notes through. However, no executive wants to argue every single note. Whether your notes meeting is in person or more likely, on a phone call, take notes and write them down as they are presented to you. You can ask your exec to email them to you as well.

If an exec tells you that something **bumped** for them, it means that something in the script disrupted their reading and bothered them. It is the equivalent of cruising along in your car and hitting a speed bump. It is essentially a nice way of saying, *I don't like this.* Your job is to take the note of what bumped, and smooth it out or fix it in your next draft.

If you are told, "I'm bumping on the mother hugging her daughter's boyfriend good-bye. Let's have her high-five him instead." This is a short way of saying, "Your character's action here is reading really inappropriate and kinda creepy, especially in the age of #metoo. So let's change it to something safe and appropriate."

Let's say that your script is about a teenage boy being sexually harassed, and somehow the exec missed that entire plotline, it is entirely fair for you to explain that. You know your story better than anyone, and you don't want to change something that pulls a thread and makes your entire plot fall apart.

What you don't want to do is discuss, explain or argue every single note that your exec gives you. It is exhausting, and no one wants to be on a three hour note call. (It happens, trust me.) You want to be a writer that execs want to work with again.

You may have heard that you should _listen for the note behind the note_. This is very true. I have given notes to writers, and had the script come back two days later. This is not a good sign. (I am referring here to notes given on early drafts. When you are working on your fourth or fifth drafts then you may be fixing a few specific lines and that will only take you a day or so.) You will most likely get the most notes on a first draft, including many general notes. Those are the ones you want to make sure you really understand and address.

Using the example above, the specific note given was to change the hug to a high-give. Easy. That is fixed in five seconds. But if you look at the note behind the note, the problem was the inappropriate behavior between an adult and a young teenager. The next step should be going through the script and changing all dialogue and actions that might also be considered inappropriate, even if the exec didn't flag every single occurrence.

Unless you are under a deadline, don't rush. You won't impress your exec by turning in a rewrite in one week rather than the three you were given. It gives the impression that you rushed through it, and that doesn't inspire confidence. If you finish your rewrite in a week, put it away for a week, then take it out again and read through it with fresh eyes. Make sure you have thoroughly addressed every note, and the note behind the note.

I like to start with the page notes and fix the easy things first, like specific lines of dialogue or action, typos, etc. Once I cross those off the list then I go back through and do the harder notes that require more time and thought. I do a pass for every broad note focusing only on that note rather than trying to fix everything at once.

If you do get a note that you can't make work, don't ruin your script trying to make it work. That is when it is a good time to email your exec to discuss that note if you choose. Your other option is not to fix it, but make sure to mention it in your e-mail when you turn in your next draft.

You know your script better than anyone, and your exec may have missed how this seemingly minor thing they want changed affects something else down the road. Again, you never want to pull a thread that makes the entire script unravel. A couple times I have had someone suggest something completely outrageous that would have changed the entire story. (Um, no thanks.) Many times people are just spit balling out loud, throwing out ideas, and trying to help. It won't help anyone's ego if I inform them that their idea is the worst, dumbest thing I've ever heard (even if it is). Instead, it is better to nod your head and respond with, "That's an interesting idea. Let me think about that." How confrontational you want to be also depends on your relationship with that particular executive. If you have made umpteen movies together, and have a solid working relationship, by all means, say whatever you want. Generally speaking though, it is just common sense not to insult the people who are working to help you get your movie made. Fight for what you believe in but choose your battles carefully/wisely.

There are many stories from the A list writers talking about how they had to fight for their projects. Sylvester Stallone fought for Rocky, and he was right! That is not usually the case for new writers though. While you may be new to this industry, your executive most likely is not and knows what is needed to get your script into sellable shape. If you feel deeply about something then fight for it, absolutely. On the other hand, we have worked with writers who refused to take notes, certain that their script was a masterpiece when in reality it had major structural issues among other problems. If they can get their project made somewhere else the way it is, the more power to them.

Creative executives will spend several hours when giving notes on a script. It takes time to read the script, make detailed notes, type up those notes, and then reread everything before the notes meeting. It is time consuming. Our goal is not to give the writer the most difficult time possible, but to help get the script into sellable shape for a specific buyer. The buyer matters because you will get entirely different story notes if your comedy is going to be for someone looking for an edgy, R rated, romantic comedy versus a family friendly romantic comedy.

The difficulty most writers have isn't usually with creative execs who understand what makes a story work, but executives who haven't studied screenwriting. Their focus may be on marketing, or making a project work for a specific buyer at a certain budget. Or perhaps a certain in-demand actor is interested but only if their part is increased, so the writer is asked to make major changes. It is up to you to decide what you are willing to do or sacrifice creatively to get your movie made.

Even if you didn't agree with all or any of the notes, be sure to thank your executive for their time and notes. Their intention is to help you get your script made. It is a win for everyone when a

141

script gets **green lit** or approved for production. That is everyone's ultimate goal.

Remember, too, that unless you are one of the few screenwriting geniuses who has the power and creative control, you want to be someone people like working with and want to work with again. If an executive has two similar projects or has an open writing assignment and needs to choose between written two equally talented writers with comparable credits, they are going to choose the writer they had a positive experience working with previously.

Revision mode:

When you start your first rewrite or the second draft, you will want to write it in revision mode.* It is a production function you can select on Final Draft. It shows an asterisk* at the end of * every line where you have made changes. It allows the exec to skim through the script and see where changes have been made. No one told me about revision mode, so I turned in the second draft of my first professional writing assignment as a clean, new draft. Oops! Save your first * draft, then save your second draft with the date as a new file. Make sure it is in revision mode.

When you turn in your script, you will want to turn it in as a PDF file. Final Draft will let you publish your script as a PDF file. Save one version with your revisions. Then save a new file * with your script, select all, and clear revision. Save that PDF as the clean version.

When you start your second revision or third draft, start with the clean version of your second * draft, and put that into revision mode. You don't continue the same revision mode because your exec will want to see the new changes that you have made on this new draft.

Some writers think the more asterisks * on a page the better, but that is not accurate. Don't play with spaces just to add more asterisks. It is too easy for execs to compare your previous draft. *

Time frame for writing drafts:

Depending on the situation and your contract, your time frame may vary, but a first draft should typically be turned in within 6-8 weeks. A second draft 4-6 weeks depending on the amount of notes you are given, and a polish, again, depending on the number of notes given, anywhere from 3 days – 2 weeks. You will need to discuss those terms and expectations with your creative development executive.

Writing in consideration of budget:

If you are writing a spec script, do not worry or limit yourself creatively by worrying about budget unless you are writing for a specific channel and you already know their parameters. Even then, you don't want to do anything that might take away from your screenplay because your goal is to get the reader or buyer to say yes to your project. After you sell your spec, or if you are hired to write on assignment, then it will be important to take budget into consideration while writing or rewriting your script.

Producers take a screenplay and break it down according to the budget. The same script can be broken down for different budgets, and then the amount of money that becomes available for the project will determine how and where it is shot, and even who is cast. If you are a writing a big budget movie (action, epic, period piece), the sky is the limit. Have fun!

If you are writing for lower budget projects like TV movies, it is helpful to be aware of what things are considered more expensive to shoot:

- Specific expensive locations. It is much more expensive to film at Bar SixtyFive at Rainbow Room in New York City than a generic bar or diner that could be shot anywhere. (Most movies are not shot in the locations they portray on screen.)

- A large number of different locations and/or very short scenes that take place in a location that only appears once in your movie. You want to utilize your locations. If you have scenes that place in a bakery, a restaurant, and a coffee shop, consider making the location one deli that serves food and coffee, and has a pastry counter.

- A large number of characters with speaking roles. Try to eliminate characters that only have one or two lines unless they are absolutely necessary. Combine characters that serve the same purpose.

- Establishing shots with people in them.

- Scenes with people walking in and walking out, which is often called *shoe leather*. It is much more expensive and time consuming to shoot a scene with a people arriving in an uber at a club, getting out of the uber, walking up to the club door then going inside the club as compared to starting the scene inside the club. In a production draft, you want to include these types of scenes only when they are essential to the story and the plot. These scenes are often the first ones to be cut in the editing room.

- Special effects (SFX)

- Visual effects (VFX)

- Computer generated imagery (CGI)

- Stunts

- Specific and expensive props that aren't essential to the plot. There is no need to write that your character is wearing a Tiffany Anniversary Blue ring unless your story is about that specific expensive piece of jewelry. (A <u>hero's prop</u> is something that is specific to your hero, and therefore important that it be exact.)

- Time periods and costumes

- Extremely long walking and talking scenes

- Extremely long driving and talking scenes

- Montages, unless you keep them in the same location

Production stages:

- Development –Writing and developing the screenplay

- Pre-production – Writing the shooting script along with attaching the director, casting, scouting locations, etc.)

- Production – Filming of the shooting script, also called principal photography

- Post-production – Editing the footage into a movie, adding effects, soundtrack, titles, credits, etc.

- Distribution – Getting the movie out into the world so people can see it!

Selling a television pilot:

If you want to sell a television pilot, in addition to the pilot you should turn in a <u>bible</u> and a <u>pitch deck</u>. The bible is a complete guidebook for your show. You will want to include information about yourself and any credits you have, an overall summary about your show, a short synopsis for each character, and a short synopsis for the rest of the episodes you have planned for the season. This shows a producer or buyer that you have enough story to last a full season should your pilot sell.

You may also want to include a pitch deck to go with your pilot. A pitch deck is a sales document that allows a potential buyer to understand the overall gist of your show. It is a condensed version of your bible but it is a sales tool so it needs to intrigue the reader/potential buyer. You can easily make a pitch deck in PowerPoint.

Here is a general guide to creating a pitch deck. You will want to include:

1) A title page

2) An overall synopsis of the show/series concept. Be sure to state what your series is, ex. 10 episodes, an hour long drama. This page is where you sell your show! If you are the director or have a director already attached, you can include a director's statement on the next page

3) A synopsis of the pilot episode, include setting

4) Season arc/short synopsis for the future episodes in the first season

5) A character look book which lists the main characters along with one or two pictures of known actors who fit the look of that character. You can put the character pages before the season arc/short synopsis if you choose.

6) A series arc if you have plans for a second season; if not, don't worry about this.

7) Sales pitch page that lists the demographics and target audience, similarly successful shows (obviously you don't want to compare your show to any programs that have failed) and any figures you have on the ratings and numbers those shows have brought in.

and lastly

8) Your bio, information, and credits

This document is a sales pitch so make sure that it is easy to read, visually appealing, and your descriptions and synopses aren't too dense. You don't want it look like the small print in The New York Times. There isn't a set rule, but pitch decks usually average from 7-15 slides. The more concise the better. Just make sure your information doesn't look too crowded.

Agents vs managers:

Many writers ask if they need an agent or a manager or both. The WGA is currently as of this writing involved in a law suit with the ATA (Association of Talent Agents). WGA writers are allowed to sign only with those agencies that are in compliance and good standing with the Guild.

Agents and managers take a 10% commission. Agents are strictly 10%, but some managers charge up to 15%. If you have both, you pay both, whether or not they worked on a specific project. If you have a lawyer, that fee is usually 5% or whatever has been negotiated between you and your lawyer.

The biggest difference is that mangers typically help guide and shape your career, and will give you feedback and notes on your scripts; whereas, agents handle your submissions and contracts. Legally speaking, managers can't negotiate deals or contracts on your behalf, but licensed and franchised agents and lawyers can.

Many companies will not take unsolicited screenplay submissions for legal reasons. If you don't have an agent or a manger, a lawyer can submit your script for you. Or you may be asked by the company to sign a standard release form.

Even if do you have an agent or a manager, you can't sit back and wait for them to make your career happen. You need to be networking (when you are not writing) and making connections. This is your career. It is up to you to be proactive to make it happen.

Advice from an agent on how to get an agent by Cary Kozlov – Cary Kozlov Literary Management

- Enter into as many screenwriting competitions as possible. Agents and managers DO pay attention to those who end up as finalists. For instance, a writer who has placed in even the Nichols Fellowship quarterfinals grabs my attention.
- Subscribe to services like VirtualPitchfest or Greenlight My Movie. I look at and respond to those pitches, and I'm mandated to respond.
- Write direct query letters – if they're lucky enough to get the agent's email address, occasionally one will jump out at me – nobody hardly sends snail mail anymore, but once in a while I get one.
- When writing email queries, keep it short and to the point! The agent doesn't have any time to read through a "novel." If it looks like that...BAM...I hit the delete button. Keep it to just a few very short paragraphs that include a logline for the project they're pitching, their credits if any, and any writing awards. If they graduated from a recognized and respected screenwriting program (e.g. USC, UCLA, Chapman University's Dodge School of Film, Cal State Northridge, etc. all jump out at me), definitely include that. For me, the subject line can very simply be "Representation Query" or something like "Action/Horror," "Broad Rom-Com," (or any other genre) "for your consideration." The agent goes through their emails very quickly. Many can have

100 emails waiting for them in their inbox. Representation queries are the lowest priority.

- DO NOT call me. First of all, I almost never answer a call if I don't recognize the number. If you do call and leave a voice-mail, make sure it's short. DO NOT leave me 3 minute voice-mails. I certainly won't listen to the entire message. That being said, once in a blue moon depending on my mood, I have been known to actually take a call or call back.

- Make sure you have at least 3 completed solid screenplays when you approach me. I won't consider representing a writer with only one completed script. It is an unwritten fact that the first script a writer goes out with will not be the magic bullet.

Dealing with rejection:

The entertainment industry isn't for the faint of heart. We all dream of being Charlie Bucket finding the golden ticket, but unless you are that one in a million whose first screenplay is a blockbuster hit, you are going to get passes on your scripts. And probably a lot of passes. It can weary the soul. Every writer knows the angst, the feeling of wanting to quit, and wondering if it is worth the time and energy and hours spent working on a script that doesn't go anywhere. It is frustrating, and it almost makes you walk away completely and find a new career altogether; one with a predictable and established path to success. You really only have one choice: quit or keep writing. If you quit, you are guaranteed to never have your screenplay turned into a movie. If you keep writing, there are no guarantees, but you are already ahead of every writer who quit yesterday, is going to quit today or will quit tomorrow. If you can't quit, no matter how frustrating and painful it feels at times, congratulations, you are a writer!

This is a true story, and shows how subjective Hollywood is: A writer and director spent nine years shopping a thriller spec around Hollywood. Everyone passed on it. Until 2019 when a fairly new and young executive read it, loved it, and green lit it for production. That thriller ended up being number one in 2020 for several days on a popular streaming service. You truly never know what can happen. So keep writing. And remember to <u>enjoy</u> your life along the way.

Your first contract:

You didn't give up, and look where you are now, getting ready to sign your first contract! I hope you are doing something special to celebrate your success!

Your agent or lawyer (managers are not legally allowed to negotiate deals or contracts on your behalf) will need to discuss your contract with you. Guild writers are protected by the WGA, but anything goes for non-guild writers. You may not earn as much as guild writers who are entitled to minimums, but since you are allowed to take writing assignments from non-signatory companies, you also have opportunities that guild members do not. There are many production companies that only work with non-guild writers. Many of them make romance, Christmas, and women in jeopardy thrillers for family friendly channels.

If your pitch is accepted and/or you are hired to write the script, a non-guild writers will often be offered <u>step deals</u>. That means you will be paid in steps like the example below.

Story treatment/outline (This is the reason why you never turn in more than 1-2 pages in the pitch phase. It is considered a step.)
Commencement of First Draft
Delivery of First Draft
Commencement of Second Draft
Delivery of Second Draft
*Polish (optional)

It is important to have in your contract what steps you are entitled to write because otherwise a production company can kick you off the project at any time and "choose to go in another direction with a new writer." This happens often so don't be alarmed if it happens to you. Screenwriting is still subjective, even when you start getting paid for your work.

If you have a company that is interested in your spec script, you may be offered an <u>option deal</u>. You will make a little bit of money up front in exchange for giving the production company a set amount of time, anywhere from 12-18 months, the option to move forward with your script. (There have been options for as low as $1 depending on the agreement with the producer.) Depending on your contract, the production company may be allowed to exercise an extension, which would pay you a little more money, and give them more time to try and make your movie. If nothing happens during the option period, the script and all rights revert back to you, and you keep all the option money.

An <u>option/purchase agreement</u> lays out the terms for your option and then the script purchase price should your movie go forward. Or your script may be bought outright without an option.

If you are offered a <u>shopping agreement</u>, usually no money is exchanged. You are simply giving a company or producer permission to exclusively shop your project around for a set amount of time. The pro side to this is that you have someone who believes in your project enough to actively be taking it out on your behalf. On the con side, you are waiting on one person to make something happen with your project, and you cannot send it out to anyone else. My understanding is that shopping agreements cannot be legally enforced, but check with your agent or lawyer.

One suggestion, always ask your agent or lawyer to get a <u>production bonus</u> included in your contract. This is a bonus you receive when principle photography either begins or ends on your project. Most producers will not have a problem with adding a production bonus because it means the movie is being made, and they are making a hefty paycheck themselves. Another possible bonus you can request is a <u>credit bonus</u>. If you are the sole writer on the project, you will receive a certain amount of money. If you end up sharing credit (which means another writer was brought in and paid to do work on the script) that original amount is often halved.

Your agent and/or manager's ten percent will be taken from the total amount before taxes, not after.

Writers who know they are guaranteed to make six figures or more a year will often form an S Corp. You will need to talk to your accountant to see if that makes sense for you.

Residuals:

Non guild writers can still earn residuals or royalties on their non-guild movies that air in certain territories overseas. Guild writers receive residuals according to the WGA terms.

Credits:

Credits are determined and arbitrated if there are any disputes by the WGA and WGC (Writers Guild of Canada) for guild members. Production companies determine the writing credits for non-guild projects. They often will not guarantee credits in your contract unless you are the original writer because it all depends on the total number of writers who end up working on a project. It is worth the blood, sweat, and tears when you see your name after WRITTEN BY on the screen!

Development hell:

You have most likely heard this term. Development hell refers to the amount of time it takes from signing the contract to actually getting your movie made. It can be months or years, even decades, and many scripts never get made at all. The ones that do may often be very different when compared to the original script that was written.

If you find yourself in this position with your project, I know it is frustrating, but you have to understand that as the writer, you have no control. "Hurry up and wait" is a common phrase in the entertainment industry, whether you are working on set, or waiting to hear back about a screenplay submission. You can continue to check in with your development executive for any new updates, but the best thing to do is to let it go and start writing your next spec script!

Movies are a collaboration:

Nobody sets out to make a bad movie, yet all too often you hear people exclaiming, "How did that get made?" Unlike the theatre where the writer is king, screenplays are considered a blueprint. Development executives give notes, producers give notes, studios give notes, the actors give notes, and the director will have notes and make changes. And that is while the movie is still in script form! Production budgets also come into play, requiring changes if certain scenes or locations are too big or too expensive to film. After a movie has finished filming, the director will turn in his cut of the movie, and then the producers will give notes on that, called the producer's cut. That version is then sent to the studio or buyer, and they will give more notes. Until finally you have what is called picture lock, which means everyone is happy with the movie scenes. The picture is locked. Then everything else, including scoring, sound, ADR (rerecording dialogue), CGI or Computer Generated Images, etc. comes together. There are many elements that have to come together in a movie, and hundreds of people who may work on it.

A writer/director will have more creative control over their project (James Cameron, Quentin Tarantino), but for writers who aren't directing their own projects, once you finish your part, you are, unfortunately, out of the process. The screenplay is completely out of your hands. You have to let it go, and trust, hope, and pray that it all works out. Don't waste your time worrying about what you can't control. It is better to get back to your computer and get to work writing your next project!

Networking and resources:

Today's on-line culture makes connecting easier than ever before. Utilize all your resources. High school and college alumni groups, writing communities and groups, and sites like the WGA, Linkedin, Infolist, Drew's Sript O Rama site, Simply Scripts, Deadline, Variety, Hollywood Reporter, Women in Film, AFI (American Film Institute), Academy of Motion Picture Arts & Sciences, and Academy of Television Arts & Sciences, Sundance Institute, and Scriptwriters Network, to name a few.

www.wga.org
https://infolist.com/
www.linkedin.com
http://www.script-o-rama.com/
https://www.simplyscripts.com/
https://deadline.com/
https://variety.com/
https://www.hollywoodreporter.com/
https://womeninfilm.org/
http://www.afi.com/
https://www.oscars.org/
https://www.emmys.com/
https://www.sundance.org/
http://www.scriptwritersnetwork.com/

Film festivals are another great way to network and get involved with the movie industry. You can attend as a guest or even better, you can volunteer! It is a fantastic way to see movies, attend panels, and meet people involved in all aspects of the entertainment industry. There is a group of theatre managers who travel from film festival to film festival across the country as a full time job.

Some of the biggest and well known festivals include (the big three/ the big five) Cannes, Berlin, Venice, TIFF (Toronto International Film Festival, and Sundance, as well as others like Slamdance, Austin Film Festival and Conference, Rotterdam, New York Film Festival, and Telluride Film Festival.

http://www.festival-cannes.com/en/
https://www.berlinale.de/en/home.html
https://www.labiennale.org/en/cinema/2020
https://www.tiff.net/
https://www.sundance.org/festivals/sundance-film-festival
http://www.slamdance.com/
https://austinfilmfestival.com/
https://iffr.com/en
https://www.filmlinc.org/nyff2019/
https://telluridefilmfestival.org/

You can find a list on-line of dozens more festivals in your area. You don't have to live in Los Angeles to get involved with the entertainment industry. Each state has a film commission you can contact. The film industry in Georgia is among the largest in the country. Many movies film in Canada, Vancouver, B.C., and Toronto, Ontario, (Toronto being the most popular).

https://www.creativebc.com/
http://www.ontariocreates.ca/film_and_tv/Ontario_Film_Commission.htm

Screenwriting contests:

Competitions are another way to get your script (and you!) noticed, and can lead to meetings with executives and agents. The most prestigious competition is The Academy's official competition, Academy Nicholl Fellowship. Sundance and Austen have respectable competitions along with numerous other competitions. The upside to contests is that it is a great way to get noticed by an agent, there are prizes for the winners, and you often get notes on your script even if you don't place. The downside is that they can be expensive if you enter many of them, and the competition can be strong.

https://www.oscars.org/nicholl

Advice from the pros:

There is no one better to learn from than those who have been where you are and are living their dreams!

MARK AMATO – Screenwriter, and Teacher at AFI, American Film Institute, 30+ titles including EARTH: FINAL CONFLICT, SUITE LIFE ON DECK WITH ZACH AND CODY, and A CHRISTMAS MIRACLE

What Happens Next?

What happens next? This would not only become a theme of my life but the most important three words every writer needs to keep in mind when breaking the story. Every scene needs to end with the audience begging the question – WHAT HAPPENS NEXT? Without that tension, your narrative falls apart. The moment you see where a story is headed, you consciously disengage.

Story is the hardest element to grasp for any writer. We're all eager to write FADE IN, but without a carefully crafted story, the train will quickly fall off the rails. I encounter many aspiring writers with half-finished screenplays tucked away in their drawers usually because of a desire to just start writing. Inevitably somewhere around page fifty, everything starts to fall apart.

Every great story starts with a great set-up. Where most aspiring writers go awry is when they lean towards the expected. They have an idea they think sounds funny when it truth it's a non-starter. An example of a non-starter set-up, I hear all the time for just about any half-hour comedy is where the lead character gets sent a chain e-mail saying "If you don't send this to ten friends, you're going to be besieged with bad luck." Guess what happens next? The character is besieged with bad things happening to him. See how it fails the "what happens next" test?

The moment the audience or reader is one step ahead of the writer; you're sunk. As I like to say, that's when the reader stops wanting to turn the page. Why turn the page if you anticipate what's coming? How many times have you sat in the theater staring up at the screen when you say to yourself, "Okay, here comes the montage?" While some may call these movie tropes, the second you see them coming, you've written a cliché.

I look at every character as an opportunity to do something fresh and unexpected. Those words will always elicit "what happens next" – and that should be the goal of every writer to bring to all aspects of their narrative. A mediocre execution of a great idea will inevitably win out over a great execution of a mediocre idea.

The most terrifying thing for a writer is the blank page. So if I am ever sitting for longer than twenty minutes with nothing coming out, I start writing questions and one-liners. What does my character want? Sometimes it may just be a riff of dialogue, a list of what-ifs or an amalgamate of movies. "Its Jaws in space." I do that then walk away and do something I enjoy—like rollerblading at the beach or hot yoga. Then something magical happens. Your subconscious starts going to work—like there's a mini-writers room inside your head. Then when you sit down at the computer—you'll have answers to the items you wrote down.

Writing should never be a labor it should always be an expression of your passion. I remember writing on <u>The Suite Life on Deck with Zach and Cody</u> with other writers complaining it's just a kid's show. But that's a hacky attitude to take, when you're lucky enough to be working on a hit show, regardless of the genre. So I endeavored to always write the BEST version of whatever show I was on or movie I had to write.

Aside from writing, I love teaching what I've learned and watching the minds of my students come alive in class. Inevitably, most of them stumble for the first several weeks coming up with non-starter stories. But I try to encourage through guiding them through their misstep to try and come up with something fresh and unique. Inevitably, most of them return with a set-up that has the class laughing. When that happens I tell them, stop digging—you've struck gold, indicating the laughter around the room. The laughter translates to the fact we're all invested in the story and we can't wait to hear the next beat. I can't tell you how many students I've had that end up delivering network quality scripts by the end of the course. I've been lucky to watch many former students get into various network fellowships, studio workshops, and even positions on staff.

I start each semester and end with the same three words written on the board. WHAT HAPPENS NEXT? If you succeed in keeping this in mind with everything you write, make sure each and every scene ends with the same question lingering in the mind of the reader, you will inevitably find success. Then with each success as your career starts to grow and opportunities begin to appear you'll be asking yourself what happens next...

NATE ATKINS – Screenwriter and Editor, 55+ titles including A CHRISTMAS PRINCE trilogy on Netflix, SINISTER SAVIOR, and CASA VITA

Don't pursue writing full time unless you really can't do anything else. It's a brutal grind. If you can do anything else, just do that instead. It really has to be the one thing you feel you need to do, otherwise, it's not worth it. The most important part is to never forget to foster the skill of enjoying the process of crafting stories. No matter how much other things can get in the way or threaten to derail it, keep the creative process joyful as much as possible because often times it's all you have. It's all about positive persistence. It's like being an actor. They put themselves out there, get rejected, pick themselves up and keep going. It's the same thing with being a writer. You'll get more passes than anything else. You have to play the numbers game. It's really common for screenwriters to become embittered. Unlike novelists where the work is the work, a screenplay is a blueprint. Many new writers think it's about just writing a script, sending it out and somebody makes it, but it doesn't work like that. Movies get made by a committee. Development executives, producers, directors, actors, everyone has an opinion. It's like being a chef in a kitchen and giving everyone something a bit to their taste. You have to be able to adapt to changing conditions both on a story level and working creatively with a team. It's a constantly changing industry and you have to be able to adapt. It's not logical, it's creative, and that's what makes our business so different. There is always some drama within the process of creating drama in Hollywood! Roll with it and stay creative. Know what your buyers want. It's a long haul. It's a one in a million chance to get an indie film that's perfect and gets a huge opening at Sunday or Cannes, and then off to the races. 99 out of 100 times, it's a long grind and you either stick with it or you don't.

ERNIE BARBARASH – Director, Producer, Screenwriter, 30+ titles including Netflix's HOLIDAY IN THE WILD, POUND OF FLESH, and AMERICAN PSYCHO

12 NOT-SO-ANGRY PIECES OF ADVICE

1. Most scripts fail at the concept/idea stage. Often the idea just isn't strong or compelling enough to carry a reader/ viewer through a 90 to 120 minute film/screenplay. As my friend Alex Epstein suggests in his great book "Crafty Screenwriting", people should really test out their idea, pitch it to other people, friends, anyone who will listen, to see if it holds anyone's interest, before taking the time to write out the whole screenplay. Just see if your idea works. I've found if you actually pitch the idea in person to someone you can really understand when you're boring them, when they're interested, etc.

   Another point to this is that people often don't spend enough time working on their idea/concept before they move on to writing the outline and then the screenplay. There seems to be some kind of misconception that people should spend most of their time writing the actual screenplay (stage directions, dialogue, scenes, etc). I think we'd all have much better movies out there if people spent more time on their idea, making sure it works, making sure it's as strong as it can be, before even starting the outline.

   Most importantly, there have to be some surprises in your story. Even if the end is predictable, the journey to get there can't be.

2. The outline. Please outline. Please know where you're heading before you start writing the screenplay – certainly before writing the scenes. It will help your scenes, your sequences,

your dialogue have PURPOSE and allow you to craft better parts that add up to a more effective whole. An outline is a skeleton, a road map, and most importantly, a tool for reviewing the story quickly, without needing to read the whole screenplay, so that you can see where the structure works and where it doesn't. Once you're writing scenes and dialogue, you start living the story through the eyes of your main characters (or at least you should be) and it will be much harder to sort out structure issues – at least try to sort out any big problems before you dive into the first draft. Again, most people don't work on their outlines enough and jump to writing scenes too soon.

By the way, this doesn't mean that the outline can't change once you start writing the draft. You may not find that something isn't working once you're on page 40 of the first draft – often you realize that you're there but you're only one quarter of the way through your outline, which means that you should probably have a faster intro to your story, a faster 1st act, something like that … And you can make changes to the story then or after you're done with the whole first draft, but again, having an outline frees you up to worry about living the story as the characters as you write them because at least for one pass you know your structure is working …

3. Please make sure that your protagonist has a series of challenges to overcome, that the challenges increase in difficulty as the story goes on, and that she or he solves the challenges in ever-more-surprising ways. Audiences love characters that surprise them with how they come up solutions that they've never thought of to tough problems, regardless of genre. Your script does not need to have a 3 act structure. That's just a shorthand way of talking about things – don't force yourself into it unless it helps you analyze your work. Beyond

that, it's pretty useless. It's more important to tell your story in a series of ever-escalating challenges to your character.

4. Try to think of what is the worst thing that could ever happen to your protagonist and what's the best thing that could ever happen to her or him and make sure both things happen during your movie.

5. Please figure out the stakes for your protagonist – the higher the better. How will their life be better if he or she succeeds at their goal, how will it be worse (and probably much much worse) if she or he fails?

6. In my experience, either your protagonist or at least someone close to him or her should have some kind of discovery about themselves, towards the end of the story. If your protagonist is just trying to solve an external problem (to rescue their kid, to find treasure, to escape from a monster, etc.), the story is not as rich as it can be. In some of my favorite stories, the heroine can't achieve their goal until she solves some kind of internal obstacles and discovers some hard truth about herself).

7. You don't need to write your outline in order of how the story unfolds. Sometimes it helps to figure out what is the climactic self-discovery or big secret reveal before most other things you write – again, so you know where you're heading and the rest of the film can be structured to get you there

8. Try to keep back something mysterious/interesting about your main character until later in the film so your audience has some reason to turn the pages to figure out what this is.

9. A format note but an important one. Try not to cram too many stage directions into one paragraph on the page and

try to find some way to break up really long dialogue sections with stage directions, even if just one person is talking. It's just easier to read it that way and reading a screenplay is often tiring on the eyes. More white space makes it easier for the reader to enjoy your story

10. Please remember that movie audience RARELY REMEMBER CHARACTER NAMES. So if it's important to your story that someone's name is very clear, make sure that it is repeated in dialogue and on screen in various ways several times before you really need for them to know what it is

11. Remember that real people rarely speak in subtext. They rarely speak out loud what they really mean or just get down to business and talk about the problem at hand. People often speak to hide truth instead of reveal it. People work very hard to project a certain image of themselves to the world, an image that may not very well be true, again, no matter the genre. Mostly, when people talk to other people in a scene, they want something from the other person. If you focus on what Character A wants from Character B in a scene and vice versa, you'll rarely have a boring scene. Finally, please try not to have your characters tell each other what they already know just because your audience needs to get this information – try to figure out another way to get this exposition across.

12. After you've finished the outline, and then once again after you finish a draft of the screenplay, I suggest you read through the whole thing and think of what scenes you DON'T NEED and whether the screenplay or outline works without them. Really, take the time and do this with pretty much every single scene in the movie. I often find that this leads to great efficiency in structure and storytelling and once you do this with the outline, you then don't waste time writing scenes that you obviously don't need.

JENNIFER BARROW – Screenwriter, Script Reader

The job of a script reader is to do just that, "read scripts". As the first stop for a spec script, script readers have a low-profile but high-impact role in the Hollywood food chain. Studios, production companies, and agencies often hire script readers to help them determine which of the many scripts they receive are worth acquiring and developing into a finished product. Readers read the scripts in their entirety (no matter how bad!) and then write "coverage" – a report on the script that usually consists of a synopsis and comments about the script's strengths, weaknesses, and potential. As part of the coverage, each script receives a Pass, a Consider, or the coveted, and rarely given, Recommend.

Just like every writer has their own process, I'm sure every reader does as well. When I read a script, the first thing I look for is a story that flows at a good pace and has a satisfying beginning, middle, and end. When the story structure works, the script works; and when it doesn't, the script has issues. I don't look for any particular structure or for something specific to happen on a certain page, but I do look for story momentum, plot points, twists, and turns. Every scene should serve a purpose and either move the story forward or reveal something important about a character. If I've read ten, twenty, or thirty pages and I still don't know what the script is about, that script has a huge problem. Also, by that far in, I should definitely feel the tone and know the genre – a romance needs to be romantic, a comedy funny, an action-adventure full of action and adventure. The script should have a lead character who is defined, interesting, and relatable. They need a clear goal, motivations, and obstacles in their way. They also need an antagonist (or antagonistic force) of some sort so they have to work/grow/change to reach their goal. A strong script also has supporting characters who enhance the story, help and/or hinder the main character, and provide a different point-of-view, and they need to be memorable and stand out from one another. Dialogue that is fresh, real-sounding, and pops off the page gets my attention. When I read description, it needs to flow, be visual, and be succinct (written mean and lean). I don't need to know what every character is wearing in every scene if it isn't crucial to the plot and you don't need to tell me that the character's bedroom has a bed, a dresser, and a closet – I already know this, I've been in a bedroom before. Screenwriters need to remember that screenplays are visual, so when I'm reading your description, I should be able to see your movie in my head. If something can't be seen on screen, it shouldn't be in your screenplay. Always reread your action and make sure every line is as strong as it can be and that it is necessary for the plot. Make sure you take the time to learn basic screenplay formatting rules. And please please please proof your script over and over … then proof it again. When I get a script that's full of typos, misspellings, and egregious formatting errors, I always think, "If this writer doesn't care about their script, why should I?" It helps when a script comes in at an appropriate length (most fall between 95-105 pages these days) as anything less than 80 or more than 120 looks amateurish. I like a title with zing, one that hints at what I'm going to read. With a pile of scripts to read, the one with the most interesting title is the one I tend to read next. If you include a logline, make sure it's good – one or two sentences that pop, are intriguing, and pull me in. If you need to tell me what genre your script is in your logline, then your script isn't ready.

Remember that the reader is your friend and a person who can help get your script made. You don't want to lose them, anger them, or waste their time with easily fixable, silly mistakes. The one piece of advice I always give aspiring screenwriters is "never submit your script to anyone until it is absolutely ready." If you're a beginning screenwriter, your first draft isn't ready, nor is your second, third, or maybe even your tenth. Screenwriting is hard … and it's much more important to write a strong script than a fast script. Readers remember the great scripts, and, just as importantly, they remember the bad ones … and the writers who wrote them.

ROBIN BERNHEIM – Screenwriter, and Exec producer, 40+ credits including showrunner for WHEN CALLS THE HEART, Co-Creator of the MYSTERY 101 series for Hallmark Movies and Mysteries, Netflix's PRINCESS SWITCH TRILOGY, STAR TREK NEXT GEN, and writer/producer for STAR TREK VOYAGER

In terms of advice … if you're a writer, it's important to keep in mind that there is no one "right" way to tell a story, only a variety of different ways. If you understand this, then it's easier to understand the process of taking notes and making adjustments. If you're a showrunner, it's important to keep in mind that it's your job to get the very best out of the people who work for you. So no matter how frustrated you are, no matter how much you'd like to yell and scream, always keep your eye on the goal, which is to motivate people to do their best work. In terms of quotes from writers I respect, the late and great Michael Gleason said this about writers don't get respect in the entertainment business: "They hate us because they can't shoot a blank piece of paper." It's still true!

BRIAN BIRD – Writer/Producer of *Captive* and Executive Producer/ Co-Creator of *WHEN CALLS THE HEART.* 40+ credits

THOU SHALT COPY
Writing Advice

Maybe you're an aspiring screenwriter or novelist. Maybe you're enrolled in an MFA creative writing program at a prestigious university. That's awesome. Good for you. Write up a storm and may your work be a force of nature, and your words change the world.

However, if you're like me, self-study may be a better choice. Don't get me wrong. I have nothing against college. In fact, I earned an undergraduate degree in journalism from a state university.

But a few years later, when I decided to morph my journalism training into screenwriting, film school wasn't an option. I was married. I had a baby boy. I had to earn a living. That's when I discovered the Best Ever Screenwriting Program in history of the universe.

It's called "Copy the Masters."

That's right, I just used the "C" word. Don't gasp. I'm not talking about plagiarism or stealing somebody else's words. Copying is the not the same as stealing.

Throughout history, here's how art has been passed down from one generation to another: Students copy their masters, but bring themselves to the canvas, marble, ceramic, celluloid, keyboard, writing page (or whatever medium you are working in) in order to eclipse their masters.

The artist William Blake said this in 1808: *"The difference between a bad artist and a good artist is the bad artist <u>seems</u> to copy a great deal. The good artist <u>really does</u> copy a great deal."*

Picture a painting class. The students are all at their easels and the teacher is at his easel at the front of the class, and what are they all doing? They are painting. The students model their work after the work of the teacher but bring their own natural gifts and muse to the process so they can surpass the skills of the teacher.

So, what does that look like for writers? What it looked like for me all those years ago was reading, reading, reading great screenplays. Epic movie scripts and teleplays by the world great screenwriting masters. I analyzed how they skinned their cats. How they paced and escalated their action and their hero's journey. How they got into a scene as late as they could and exited as early as possible. How they made their conflict rise and not jump. How they made me fall in love with their characters.

And then I just started mimicking them. Not copying their words but letting them prime my writing pump by inspiring me with how they accomplished their goals. It made me jealous of their craft and beckoned me to try to show them up with my skills. A little secret: After 35 years of doing this work, and somehow making a consistent living at it, I still read five great screenplays before I begin each new project. It's the only way I feel I can get better at what I do. And that should really always be our goal … to strive for excellence and show ourselves approved.

Contemporary Texas artist Bill Herring has this to say about the imitation game:

"In every art class, the fastest way to learn has always been to copy. You get around someone, you learn what they know, and then you disengage from them and go find tutors who are strong where your mentor is weak. You then become better than your teacher. Do not be afraid of copying. In fact, the mark of a great student is a student who can copy. Learn everything you can about what your mentor knows, then add what you know and become better than your mentor."

Okay, so what if you're a novelist? Or a sportswriter? Or you write human-interest features for your local newspaper. Or you've launched your blog to try to share your wisdom and scintillating wit with the world? What master will you be copying?

Well, that's where you need to do some homework in order to identify who your teachers will be. I only have one rule: Choose world-class mentors in whichever field you are working. Not your Aunt Tippie and her unpublished, vanity novel. Sorry, Aunt Tippie.

Happy copying.

JANEEN & MICHAEL DAMIAN – Actors/Singer/Writers/
Directors/Producers 115+ titles including HIGH STRUNG FREE
DANCE on Netflix, HIGH STRUNG, CROWN FOR CHRISTMAS,
and FLICKA: COUNTRY PRIDE

JANEEN: I would say the first thing is know your ending.

MICHAEL: Yes!

JANEEN: We also like to name all of our main characters before we
start so that we can immediately have—

MICHAEL: —a relationship with them.

JANEEN: Yes. Every team writes differently. We do everything col-
lectively. We don't parcel anything out. We use screen share,
and have one person on the computer typing. The document always stays with that one person. We read the dialogue
together, always.

MICHAEL: I drive Janeen crazy because I like to push forward every
day and not go back and rewrite scenes from the day before.
I like to get to the end, and then we can go back to the beginning. Otherwise, if you go back every day then you tend to
not push the story forward. We like to keep the momentum
and the arc of the story moving, and let that keep fueling us.
Instead of reverse-forward, reverse-forward.

JANEEN: Michael doesn't believe in writer's block. He won't even
let me say the word.

MICHAEL: You just said it! That freaks me out! Ear muffs, ear muffs,
ear muffs, ear muffs!

JANEEN: (laughing) Writing is a job, and like any other job, you
can't just decide that you don't feel like showing up that day.
You have to show up and write every day.

MICHAEL There are good days and bad days in any work. Some
days you're motivated and some days you're not.

JANEEN: We set a deadline of 5 pages a day. At least 5 pages.

MICHAEL: I go through the calendar and I map the whole thing
out to the finish. It's a great psychological tool to set your
goals. You want to have the first draft done by this day, and

then you can go back and do your polish. It gives you a nice visual reminder.

JANEEN: If you get off track, you know you need to pick it. For instance, action sequences or dance sequences take up very little space on the page, but take a long time to write. So there are always those variables. Anything else, Michael, that you want to share?

MICHAEL I did, but I just had writer's block on it.

JANEEN: (laughing)

MICHAEL: I learned this as a singer, record producer where I would work on a song, listening to it over and over, remixing, and then you kind of get sick of it. You have to remember what excited you about the script from the beginning. Especially when you get discouraged, or you may not be excited as you're going through it. Believe me, get it done. Get to the end. Trust that instinct you had when you first decided to write the script. Stay with it and don't let it leave you, because many things can lead you away or distract you. Also, be careful about other people's opinions as far as who you let read your script. Be very selective before you send it out into the world. Don't you think?

JANEEN: Yes, then after it's been submitted, keep a very open mind to notes. Listen to [the buyer] you're selling it to because they know that market better than anybody.

MICHAEL But hold onto that vision of what you intended in the beginning. You have to hold onto the story and characters that you created, and why you wrote it in the first place.

JANEEN: The other thing is that as a team, we agree to always agree. So if one of us disagrees about something, we just keep working through it until we both agree and then move forward.

MICHAEL: Yep.

JANEEN: That way you always have the harmonious atmosphere when you're writing. We're very collaborative that way. We always make sure that we're both happy with the direction that everything is going in.

MICHAEL: Listen to the characters because they actually tell you
what to do, day to day.
JANEEN: We wish you the best of luck!

Rock on!

TIPPI AND NEAL DOBROFSKY – Screenwriters, 40+ credits including Netflix's HOLIDAY IN THE WILD, LOVE IN WINTERLAND, and Hallmark's WEDDING MARCH movie series

Keep believing in yourself, no matter what.

And write every day. Simple and obvious I guess but that's what got us through hard times. There were a lot of years when we were dead broke and we always said, "We just have to write our way out of this."

It's not an easy lifestyle. You have to love writing more than you love making money or having security. Because it will be a rollercoaster for sure.

ADAM FINER – Professor of Screenwriting at New York Film Academy, Producer and Consultant (former Universal Studios Market Research Executive and former Literary Manager)

This advice may sound like 'write what you know,' just from a different perspective, but the truth is, most of us don't know anything that interesting. And so new writers tend to write what they think we want. They tend to write what they think the industry wants, and they shouldn't. Stop writing things that you think we want and write what you have to say. Stop writing movies about Hollywood. Stop writing the period piece that has little chance of getting made. If that's the story you have to tell, tell it, but understand that your experience and your background have to play so heavily into that. 'Write what you know' doesn't mean write another comic book movie that you don't have control of, that you don't have the rights to, that nobody is going to buy because there are enough comic books out there for them to option. Write from your experience, from your passion from your personal voice, and you'll find something compelling to say and you may find the right person to say it to.

On a common pitching mistake: I see this with a lot of students and even professionals, make sure that your pitch matches the tone of your project. If you're pitching a romantic comedy, please have some humor, romance and some fun in your pitch and your pitching style. If you're pitching an action drama, please have some action and some drama in your pitch. Don't pitch your comedy as if it's a dark dramatic project. Make sure that your tone matches your pitch.

ADAM FROST –Writer/Co-Executive Producer for TRIBAL, and staff writer for CASTLE

Everybody has a different path. I would say first and foremost, <u>write</u>. I know it sounds simple, but writers write. I think a lot of times people get swept up in meetings and agents and breaking in, but the strongest tool someone has to "break through" is having a really good sample that they're really proud of, that somebody can vouch for and say, "Hey, this is really good, you should read this person." And ideally hire them at some point. I feel like that's one of the strongest arrows in the quiver.

Build up a network of like minded, positive other writers because chances are you will be working for another writer. I think it helps when people surround themselves with positive and like minded souls who are trying to tell stories. At the end of the day, writers hire writers. The more people that you can get to know and trust, the better. The way I broke in was by doing some very simple grunt work. I was an intern on The Walking Dead. I was schlepping coffee. I was a writer's PA when I was almost 30 years old. I was happy doing it, even though it was grunt work, getting lunches, making sure the coffee was there, and wiping the boards. It's not glorious work, but it got me in the room. That was my path. I recommend getting to know as many writers as you can.

Writers' rooms are all different. On one hand, it's a very basic situation, which is a room with a white board or a cork board or screen with all the information about an episode, a conference table and a whole bunch of writers around it pitching ideas, and trying to break story.

Every show is different. On some shows the showrunner will assign episodes. On other shows all of the episodes are written together or even in the room itself. More so in comedy where there are jokes and the script is up on the board, and the writers go joke by joke through the script — so I'm told as I've never worked in a straight up comedy room. Comedy rooms are a bit of a different animal than typical dramas. On the dramatic shows that I've been on, the showrunner and the staff collaborate on the big moves in the story outline, and then the writer assigned by the showrunner goes off and writes the actual scenes/actions/dialogue. Inevitably that gets filtered through the showrunner or senior writers who will probably take a pass, and say, "Okay, great work, I'll take it from here." If you're a junior writer, chances are your writing is going to be reworked quite a bit.

I like the collaborative nature of TV writing. It's fun being in a room with diverse people, especially because writing is itself so singular, and you're in your head all the time. Like any job, sometimes you get frustrated and you just can't figure out the problem, but it is really helpful and amazing to be able to bounce ideas off people. Sometimes you'll pitch something and people might not respond but the flip side is sometimes you'll pitch something you think is terrible and people will say, "I love that idea!". By and large, it's a really cool job.

People tell you to write what you know. There is value in that, but the fundamental thing is to write what excites you. It's important not to chase the market. Be aware of it and understand it, but at the end of the day, the scripts that get noticed tend to be the ones that really come from the heart. When you are excited, that reads on the page rather than someone who just wants to write something flashy they think will sell. Especially starting out, because you're going to be at such a disadvantage. It is going to be a lot harder to crack that nut trying to write a popular show, than if you come up with something that is a little more personal. Write what you're excited about rather than chasing the market.

TED HUMPHREY – Television & Film Screenwriter, Produce, Director, Creator – THE LINCOLN LAWYER, INCORPORATED, THE GOOD WIFE, WISDOM OF THE CROWD

This is something I get asked about so often. I speak to groups of students from my various alma maters (WRA, Georgetown, UVA) or to young people trying to break into the industry. And the question they all want answered is: how do you break into the industry? Unfortunately, it's the hardest question to answer, because there is no set path. It's not like medicine or law, where you go to school and get a piece of paper and then you can apply for a job. People say it's about who you know, not what you know. And while there is some truth to that, I think it's a combination of both.

I'll give you an example to explain what I mean. When I first moved to LA to try and break into Hollywood, back in the dark ages of the late 1990's, I knew almost no one. Actually I knew one person – Jeff Schaffer. And I slept on his couch (he was already a working tv writer, writing on Seinfeld) and I wrote screenplays and tried to get people to read them. And I did coverage for Imagine and some other production companies, and did various other jobs to pay the rent. I was also toying with being an actor, and I did some plays in small theaters around LA and some short films that nobody ever saw, and so forth.

After about a year and a half of this, I got a break. I had a good friend, who had a friend, who we used to hang out with. Now this guy (my friend's friend) was maybe the sketchiest guy I knew. He was a trust fund kid from New York, who had directed a short film that had gotten into Sundance and gotten him some attention. And he'd worked for a while as an assistant to a big director. He was a good guy and fun to hang out with, but he was pretty much a dilettante – I haven't heard from this guy in 20 years. He has since directed a couple of movies, neither of which ever did anything, and I'm pretty sure he's back in NY working for the family real estate business or whatever.

Anyway, this guy looked at me one night when we were out drinking or whatever, and said: "Hey, you're trying to be an actor. You should meet with my friend who manages actors." I said sure – I would meet with anybody, anytime. So I met with his friend. His friend was a legit manager, but he mostly represented young comedians and tried to get them parts in sitcoms. I was as far from a comedian as one could be – I wrote, and wanted to act in, dramas. So while he was willing to represent me, it didn't seem like much would come of that.

BUT – he said "Hey, you're a writer, too. And you used to be a lawyer (because I practiced law in D.C. for two years before giving it up to come try to be a screenwriter). You should meet with my best friend, who's a manager who represents writers. He has a lot of clients who used to be lawyers, and he gets them jobs on legal tv shows."

Again, I said "sure!" And I met with his friend. Who turned out to be a very reputable manager named Larry Shuman. He read my feature scripts, and he thought they were good. But he was honest with me that he really didn't represent a lot of feature writers – most of his clients worked in TV.

At that time, I'd given no thought to working in television. I was here to write and direct movies. But Larry said to me "Have you ever written a TV spec script?" (At that time, the "spec episode of a show," rather than the now-ubiquitous "spec pilot," was the usual calling card in TV.) I said no. He said "Come back to me when you've written two of them."

So I went off. I didn't even watch much TV, so I had to think about what shows I even knew well enough to write. I finally settled on LAW AND ORDER and THE X-FILES. And in six weeks, I wrote a spec of each. I gave them to Larry, who later told me he assumed they wouldn't be any good because I'd written them so quickly. Nonetheless, he read them and felt they were good. He agreed to represent me. Within a month, he'd gotten me meetings at all the major agencies, and I signed with what was then the William Morris Agency (what is now WME).

Once at William Morris, I went out for TV jobs. I didn't get any that first staffing season. But then my new feature agents at the agency took out one of my spec features that I'd written. It didn't sell, but a lot of producers and studio execs liked it (there was no Blacklist at the time, but it made the unofficial list of "best" scripts that floated around back then). So it got me a lot of meetings on different projects, and out of that, maybe 6 months later, I got my first paying writing gig: doing a rewrite on a big sci-fi action movie for Warner Brothers. Then, the following TV staffing season, I got my first job as a staff writer on a TV show. Now, 22 years later, I've never been unemployed as a writer in Hollywood. For the last 8 years, I've been under an overall deal at a major TV studio, creating and running TV shows.

What's the moral of the story? Basically, it's what I started with: it's both WHO you know and WHAT you know (or what you can do, anyway). And WHO you know might surprise you. On some very real level, I owe my entire career to the sketchiest, most random guy I knew, who just happened to introduce me to a manager who just happened to introduce me to another manager, who was actually willing and able to help me. That's the WHO part. And I'd like to think that if it hadn't been that connection, then I still would have broken in via some other connection. But who knows how long that might have taken?

Either way, the WHAT part is equally important: when opportunity finally knocked, I was ready. I'd written several good feature scripts. Good enough that when my new feature agents took one of them out, it almost sold, and while it didn't sell, it helped me get the job that launched my career. And on the TV side, while I'd never written a TV spec script, I was able to write two good ones in 6 weeks.

Cara J. Russell

Why? Because I'm so talented? Well, I'd like to think talent is part of it. But at least as big a part of it is that I'd put in the work to learn my craft. For almost two years I did nothing but write, and work whatever jobs I had to do to support that writing. So that when I was asked to write those scripts, I was ready to do so, in a very compressed time frame.

Basically, everyone's career requires talent, hard work, and luck. In probably equal measures. Of course you have to have talent – that's a given. But talent without hard work is useless. And unfortunately, talent and hard work without luck isn't much use either, or it's going to take a very long time, anyway. Luck is when a random person you know introduces you to someone who introduces you to someone who can help you. Talent and hard work are when, having met that person, you actually have material you can give them that's good, that can help you. Because without that material, meeting that person will be nothing but a wasted opportunity.

So my advice to fledgling writers is: A) write, write, write, and write some more. Develop both your talent, and your work ethic. And then B) meet everyone you can, because you never know which person you meet or contact you make might be the one that can actually help you.

But you can't really game that system. Everybody knows the person whose eyes are roaming around the cocktail party, looking for someone more important to talk to. And nobody likes that person. My situation worked because the person who was able to help me was doing so because we were actually friends, not because I was trying to use him to get somewhere (in fact I had no idea he knew anyone who could help me, and really he didn't – he knew someone who knew someone).

It's the most frustrating part of the business, honestly, because there is no real way to game it. You just have to do everything possible to make yourself ready, and then keep putting yourself in the position where hopefully that readiness will meet with an opportunity.

Nowadays, of course, you can also help yourself via the many online script competitions and so forth that exist. When I was trying to break into Hollywood, the internet was still in its fledgling state. There was very little in the way of online resources. Now you can find the script for any movie or tv show you like on the internet and read it for free. Back then, you had to know someone who had an agent to get your hands on a script. They were like gold. You read somebody's copy of a copy of a copy of "Se7en," so faded you could barely make out the words, to try and glean some insight about how to structure a script or "what would sell."

Also back then, it was really hard to make a film. There was no digital video to speak of. You needed film and cameras and stuff that cost a lot of money. A short film might cost 25k to make, or more. It was beyond the financial means of most aspiring filmmakers (unless they were trust fund kids, like my sketchy friend). Now, you can shoot a film for free on your phone. And it will look better than that film somebody spent 25k to make back in 1998. The barriers to entry are a lot lower now. But, correspondingly, I think even more people are trying to break in. So it's probably a wash, all in all. Easier to get through the door, but maybe more competition once you get there. Hard for me to say which system is better. And truthfully, there was always a lot of competition, unless you go back to the 1930's or something. But what I can say is what I said above: put yourself in a position to be ready to open the door when opportunity knocks. That's what you have to do. In many ways, it's all you can do. But it's the most important thing you need to do.

Cara J. Russell

AMY KRELL – EVP of Production at Motion Picture Corporation of America, 85+ movies

Go to law school instead!

In theatre, you cannot change a line. TV is a producers' medium with showrunners as head writers. Movies are a directors' medium. They are the boss, they are god. When you write a screenplay, it becomes the bible. It is the guidebook, there is nothing else. When you are writing to sell a script that is a very different beast than writing a shooting script. I feel very strongly about not limiting yourself in the writing process. It's only when you're writing on assignment that you have to start thinking about limiting yourself. There are two scripts, the script you're going to write, and the script I'm going to make for production on set so nothing gets missed. I'm a big format person. Don't manipulate the page count. Don't screw with the margins. Do not try to cheat the spaces, font, etc. I will know, and you're not doing anybody any favors. Edit your script. Everyone overwrites. You've got to figure out how to tell your story in a certain amount of time. Scripts should be 100-105 pages in my reality. You have to kill your darlings. That's what I have to do every day in my life, kill everybody's darlings. It's so hard! You should watch movies that are like the one you want to write. If you want to write a Mission Impossible like movie, watch a Mission Impossible movie. If you want to write a Hallmark movie, watch Hallmark movies. Count how many locations there are, the number of characters with speaking roles, and see where they're shooting. Try making a movie on your phone that you direct yourself. You will learn how to limit stuff when you have to figure out how to shoot it yourself!_

191

AMANDA PHILLIPS – EVP of Original Content and Acquisitions, Motion Picture Corporation of America, and Executive Producer, 220+ titles

9 Tips for Aspiring Writers

1. Make a writing schedule and stick to it.
2. Working a day job is totally normal.
3. Write what you know or inspires you and most importantly what you can have fun with!
4. Read other writers' screenplays – may it be an Academy Award winner or a novice.
5. Continue to educate yourself in all forms of writing, especially storytelling. Take classes, join writing groups and sign up for workshops.
6. Be collaborative – with executives, producers, directors, etc. – they will help make or break your career.
7. Go outside of your comfort zone – you might find that you are a better horror writer than you ever imagined.
8. Take care of your mental and physical health and keep things in perspective – this will help avoid burn out. (I.e. don't let yourself get too high or too low.)
9. Pay attention to and take cues from what's been successful in the marketplace, but always have your own unique spin – always try to reinvent the genre you're working with, or create a new twist or spin.

Bonus Tip – adopt a dog or cat for support – they are a writer's best friend!

Cara J. Russell

ROMA ROTH – CEO/President RWM Inc. (Reel World Management) and Executive Producer of the Netflix Original Series VIRGIN RIVER as well as Producer, Screenwriter and Director

It's important to read as many scripts as you can to get a sense of what works and what doesn't and learn about structure, character and dialogue. Scripts for existing shows and pilots are available on the internet so you can purchase them for a nominal fee. These are a great learning strategy. I honed my craft by watching a lot of movies and reading thousands of screenplays. You can't sit down and think you're going to be able to write a perfect screenplay without doing your homework and analyzing the structure of the type of screenplay you're writing. Whether it's a pilot or a TV movie, each script has its own structure and things evolve and change. For example, with SVOD and AVOD platforms the scripts need to be binge-worthy so you will need to ensure you have cliffhangers after every act. Broadcaster needs change too depending on how many commercial breaks they need. So you need to research the current trends to know which structure you are writing for.

Secondly you should understand the marketplace and how marketable your idea actually is before writing it. You don't want to waste your time writing a passion project that no one's ever going to produce.

When I acquired the rights to the Virgin River novels, I spent six months actively looking for a book series that I believed would not only be adaptable but would also resonate on an emotional level with an audience. I was looking for something I felt was not already on the air. To do this you need to do your research in the US and Internationally so that you can be ahead of the curve as you anticipate where the industry will be going. As we live in a world that is currently changing you need to be aware of everything that affects what people are watching. From politics, and news to the economy – it all influences what broadcasters and platforms are programming.

In regards to staffing, I look to see who is the right fit for our projects. Who brings the right voice for the characters and the genre and can connect deeply with the material. When you're running a room, the big thing is to oversee the creative direction of a show and the story you are telling, not just that season but where the show will go over the course of many seasons to ensure longevity. Then you want to add writers to the room that bring their own unique voice and reflects the diverse world that we live in now. To do this, you need to have a balanced room made up of writers with different life experiences who each bring something unique to the table. The room should include a variety of voices i.e. male, female, LGBTQ, younger and older as well as culturally diverse because you should be creating and portraying a world that is representative of the world we live in today. Audiences are influenced by what they watch, so be aware that what you create will guide and influence and inspire the audience. Help create a narrative that positively impacts the world we live in today.

Another important point is learning to be collaborative and developing a thick skin. You can't take things personally in this business. Though I know being a writer ultimately means that you are exposing yourself emotionally to other people, you need to be ready for the fact that not everyone will like or agree with what you write. So you need to know how to take criticism and be a writer that is easy to work with. It's important to remember that there are a lot of different voices and opinions that go into a production, so you need to learn to make changes and be flexible.

And it's important to keep in mind that sometimes your script might not resonate with someone, but it could with another. So be open to learning why your script isn't working for someone and ask them to tell you what they didn't like about it. Was it the structure, the characters, the dialogue or perhaps they just didn't like the subject matter? Then keep revising and reworking based on the constructive feedback.

You should be aware that executives are inundated with scripts and are very busy so some may only read the first ten pages of your script and if it doesn't grab them, they won't continue reading.

And finally take the time to distance yourself from your script and set it aside after you write it so that you can review it with fresh eyes. Doing this will allow you to see things you didn't notice the first time around when you may have been too close to the material.

At the end of the day the most important thing is to never give up on yourself and your dream. If you want to be a writer you'll need to keep reading, learning, developing and off course writing and you can never take no for an answer. At the end of the day, you need to be the one to believe in yourself, despite what anyone else says.

BRIAN SAWYER & GREGG ROSSEN – Screenwriters, 30+ credits including Hallmark's CROSSWORD MYSTERIES series, and CHRISTMAS IN ROME

We met at USC film school and collaborated on our student films... then after graduation started writing spec scripts, and eventually got a manager and sold a pitch. We started writing mainstream comedies and sold a couple of feature spec scripts that never got made. But in the meantime we decided to adapt some of our feature scripts to TV and sold one to Hallmark, and from there realized that TV was a much faster way to get things made. Since then we've continued in both film and TV.

On Writing Partnerships:
Usually, we collaborate remotely— online or by phone. When we're developing our own projects, we'll brainstorm lots of ideas, and see if one "sticks." If it does, then we'll write up an outline and pass it back and forth over email till we're happy with it. (For us, a good idea is one in which ideas for scenes and structure come easily... if we really have to wrestle with it, or if it doesn't seem fun, then the idea may not be the best to pursue.) Then we divide up the outline, write scenes, and later paste them all together. And then gradually (over weeks and months) we smooth it out and make it flow into a coherent script. Other comedy duo friends of ours have totally different processes— actually writing in the same room— so there's no one way that people seem to do it.

General Thoughts:

- Write for a set period of time every day— whatever your schedule and other commitments will allow— just like it's a job, because that's what you want it to be.

- If you feel like your writing isn't so good...just keep at it. As with all things, it takes time and practice, and most people's first scripts aren't great (though maybe yours will be).

- After you finish a first draft, put it aside for a couple of weeks and then come back to it with fresh eyes. It will help you see places where you can improve it, or clarify things.

- After you finish your first script, write another, and then another. The more you write, the better you'll get. And the more samples you have, the greater the chance one of your scripts will fit what someone else wants.

- A writing partnership is great, especially if you like to bounce ideas off someone else. But some advice...if one person says that he or she is just the "idea person" coming up a concept, while the other one can do the actual writing...be careful. Coming up with an amazing idea is maybe 1% of the effort, the other 99% is working the story every day.

- Understand three-act story structure. Even if you want to re-invent the medium, learn what has worked for generations so you can identify how (or if) you want to be different. Good luck.

DAVID S. WARD – An Interview with Academy Award Winning Screenwriter, Director, and Professor at Chapman University's Dodge College of Film and Media Arts – THE STING (Academy Award winner for Best Original Screenplay), MAJOR LEAGUE, SLEEPLESS IN SEATTLE, among 45+ titles

What advice or words of wisdom do you have for new writers about writing in general?

The most important thing about writing is to actually do it. You learn more from writing than you do reading about writing. You learn how you work best. You learn what works for you as opposed to what you think should work for you. The more you write, the better you are at finishing what you write. It's very important to finish what you write. A lot of people will start an idea and they'll give up halfway through because they hit a difficult point. In every script you ever write, you're going to hit a difficult point. There's no script that's ever been written that didn't have a difficult point. As a writer you have to learn how to get through those points. Otherwise, you'll never finish a script. And if you don't finish a script, you won't ever sell one. Nor will you learn from the one you stopped writing. The first thing is to write and finish what you write. Even if doesn't turn out exactly like you want it to, even if you don't think it's great, it's important to finish because it helps you develop the discipline to do so.

I, quite frankly, have never read a book on screenwriting. I did go to film school, and I concentrated mostly on directing. It wasn't until I was in my last year of film school that I started to write. I've tried to read books on screenwriting, but they drive me crazy because they all take the position that if you do this and this, you will be successful. There is no magic bullet when it comes to screenwriting. There are things that you should know that will help you become more efficient, and will help you understand what you're trying to do, but there is no formula for success. You have to have a certain instinct, a certain talent, and you have to be relentless. You have to be determined and keep with it. I've had a lot of jobs in my life, but I've never had a job that's harder than writing. It may not be terribly hard physically, but mentally it's very difficult. You have to be alone. It's not a social activity. You have to learn how to discipline yourself, keep yourself from crippling self-doubt, and persevere when things might not be going well. Part of being a being a writer is understanding what's involved in writing. You don't sit down every day and write wonderful stuff. Some days you have no ideas, some days you have to rely on craft, and other days you are truly inspired.

One of the most important things for new writers is to understand what you're trying to do. What your characters want. People sometimes try to write scripts about ideas or themes, and they wind up writing characters that do everything that the theme requires. Those aren't real characters. Those are cogs in the wheel. When I write, I start with characters. I want to know, who this is about, what they want, and why. The question you have to ask is, what do your characters want and why should I care? You can write about something a character wants, but if nobody cares whether the character gets it or not, you're not going to be successful. You're not going to sell the script. You have to learn to write about characters who want things that are interesting and intriguing to people. Even things that may not be something that most people reading the script would necessarily want themselves. But if they're interested enough in the character and why the character wants it, then they'll continue to read.

As a writer you have to understand that a script is a selling tool. You're trying to tell a story with characters that appeal to the people who can actually get it done – directors who want to direct it, actors who want to play the part, to people who want to finance it because they feel like there will be other people who will be interested in it. You have to keep those things in mind as you're writing. I'm not saying you have to pander, but you have to write about things in a way that will be compelling to other people. As a writer, you have to be interesting. If you're not interesting, your stuff is not going to be bought. It's not going to be made. How to be interesting? You have to go deeply into the world of your characters. You have to know more about the characters than you have time to write in the script. It's always better to know more and not use it all. Or you may use it in a way that is more subtext than overt.

I often tell screenwriters to take a course in acting. That's where I learned how to write. I studied acting at the Lee Strausberg Institute for a year. I didn't want to be an actor, but I learned how actors break down scenes and characters so that they can play them in a way that's real. The way that actors break down and look at characters, and the questions they ask about characters are the same questions that writers should be asking themselves as they write those characters. Not only will that take them deeper into the character, they will write characters that appeal to actors. That was my education in screenwriting, acting. Like I said, I've tried to read books on screenwriting, but I felt that they're all too formulaic. I learned about writing through learning about characters and how actors look at character and break character down.

What actors generally want in a character, the essential thing they want to know, and what most screenwriting books and teachers will tell you is, you have to know what the character wants. Now, what the character wants is not necessarily what the character needs, but they have a reason for wanting it. You have to know why they want it. You have to know what the obstacles are going to be in getting it. This thing they want, it doesn't have to be something outside of themselves. It may be something personal. Perhaps they want to be perceived or look at themselves in a different way, or they want to feel better about themselves. It's not always about winning the big game, getting revenge, or having some huge goal that they achieve. Those are things you can write about, but it doesn't always have to be that. You need to know what your characters want. Once you have a character that is intriguing to you, then put that character in a situation that will explore all of that character's problems, idiosyncrasies, strengths, weaknesses, loves, hates, and so on.

You need to know what the major conflict is, the problem your character has in getting what they want. If the story is about them trying to get what they want, they don't have it yet. If they don't have it yet, there are reasons they don't have it yet. We should be somewhat aware of what the biggest obstacle to them is within the first 20-25 pages.

People need to know what they're going to be dealing with in your story. There will be more obstacles that reveal themselves as you go on with the script, but you have to establish early on what your major characters want and what their biggest problem is in getting it. You can add other problems and expound on those problems later, but if you don't establish the biggest obstacle within the first 20-25 pages, people reading the script, particularly professional script readers looking for material, are not going to read much further. You've got to hook them, and you've got to do it early. You can't hook them 55 pages in. They're not going to wait 55 pages. You've got to hook them early.

When I'm talking to writers, there are four questions I have them ask themselves:

1. Who are the characters, and what do they want?

2. Why should I care?

3. What stands in the way of the characters getting what they *want?

   *This is different from what they may need. Sometimes a character in a movie gets what they need instead of what they want, which can be just as satisfying. Sometimes characters want things that aren't good for them, or they haven't really thought it though. Or they haven't had enough experience to understand that what they want is not what they need.

4. What do you want me to feel and think after I've read your script? i.e. What are you trying to do? Where do you want to have taken me emotionally or intellectually? Do you want to educate me in some way? Why did you decide to do tell this story instead of a million others you could have told?

You want students to be able to answer those questions. If they can't answer those questions, then they haven't thought enough about what they're doing to actually do it. After they've finished the script, they should be able to answer, why did you decide to tell your story this way?

I have to have answered those four questions for myself before I can start writing. And then once I start writing, then I go where that takes me.

When someone asks your secrets to writing an Academy Award winning script, what do you tell them?

Again, there's no secret to it. You write the best script you can, and if you're fortunate enough, you write a script that appeals to enough people. When I was writing THE STING, I didn't know it would be an Academy Award winning script. I was just trying to tell a good story with characters that people hopefully cared about. You can't set out to write an Academy Award winning script. If I knew how to do that, then that's all I'd write! It's a matter of the right story at the right time. You have to be a little bit lucky. And for whatever reasons, it has to fit into a certain zeitgeist at the time. The same movie two years before or two years after may not win the Academy Award. It may not even be a hit. These are things that are out of your control. You don't write for awards, you write to write the best script you can. You write to write a script that you feel strongly about and believe in, because you'll do a better job of writing that script than one that you don't.

Where do you get your ideas, and how do you make your ideas into such great scripts/movies?

I usually tend to start from character. Although with MAJOR LEAGUE, I started from the idea that if I don't write a movie where the Cleveland Indians actually win a division title, then they never will during my lifetime. So, I said, okay, it's got to be a comedy because obviously they haven't won. Then I started thinking, what kind of characters would be in this movie? What kind of characters would this team be made up of? I took those characters from baseball players that I knew or that I read about, and combined the qualities of some of them into characters. I tried to have a range of characters that were all different, but each one had some aspect of a real baseball problem about them and/or a real personal problem about them.

So your ideas come from your own experiences, what you read, from people you know, or wish you knew. They come from who you are, or who you wish you were. I've never written anything that was autobiographical, at least, certainly not intentionally. I always hope my characters are more interesting than I am. You get characters from just interacting with people, from reading articles, books. Sometimes you get a character idea from watching other movies or television, something you observe, and so on.

To me, writing is a process of taking a character and creating the world around that character, and then taking them through a specific problem or set of circumstances toward a goal, and then seeing what happens when they either reach that goal or they don't reach that goal.

When I write a script I don't do cards or an outline. I start with a basic character, and then I start to think about a basic story. I think about how I want it to end before I even start to write it. A lot of times the ending will change because I'll get a better idea as I'm writing the character and putting the story together. I don't ideate a whole story and then write it. I know that's not very helpful for most writers because that's not very specific, but it's the way I do it. I have an end in mind, and I know what I want the end to be. I know why I want it to end that way. I know what I want people to feel from the movie. As I go along the end may change a bit, but how I want them to feel doesn't. I can't start writing unless I know where I'm going. I have to write towards a target, and if I don't have that target then I don't have a way of knowing whether a scene I'm writing is going in the right direction or whether it's a dead end, or going off in some direction that will never pay off. When you're a professional writer, you can't afford to do that. You have to be more efficient than that. I always know where I want to end, and it can change while I'm writing, but I write toward that end. Along the way I have certain anchors, scenes that do this and this. I lay those scenes out like breadcrumbs along the way to the end. When I get to those scenes, I sometimes do something slightly different with them because the character has developed in a slightly different way than I thought.

Character is one of the things [my students] have trouble with because character is much more abstract than structure. Anybody can learn structure, but inventing characters is more difficult than inventing story. If you invent a character and the character is not complex enough, or you don't understand the character well enough, it'll stop talking to you sometime during the script and then you're dead. You're going to hit the wall. When that happens, you have to dig deeper into the character or up the stakes for the character. Do something that moves the character off of where it is because otherwise you just staring at a wall.

Writing is difficult, it's not easy. It's taxing. It requires thinking. It requires concentration and dedication. It requires not letting yourself be distracted. The most important thing when you're writing the script is staying in the zone of it.

Often when I start to write a script, I have a piece of music that I associate with what I think the feeling of the script is, and encapsulates the feeling that made me start writing this movie about this character. MAJOR LEAGUE, I had this image that started with the character of Wild Thing, and I had the song "Wild Thing" in mind. I had a song for Wesley Snipes' character, too. I thought the opening of Van Halen's "Ain't Talkin' Bout Love" was the music I would play over Willie Mays Hayes stealing a base. For THE STING, one of the songs was the Eagles' "Take It to the Limit" and a couple blues songs. SLEEPLESS IN SEATTLE, one song of many was Sinatra's "One For My Baby (and One More For the Road)." On that, I was doing a rewrite. When I get bogged down or if I get stuck, I'll play that piece of music and it puts me back where I started. It reminds of what I was trying to do, and what kind of feeling I was working toward. It helps reorient and rejuvenate me.

On the business of screenwriting

As a writer you have to be aware of the business. If you have 3 or 4 different ideas, you have to be aware of the cultural zeitgeist to know which of them may be the most relevant. Why write something that you know doesn't really fit what's happening at the time? Although, what's happening in popular culture can change. What you don't want to do is chase hits. Just because somebody has written a certain kind of movie doesn't mean you want to write something in that same vein. By the time your script is finished, that vein may have passed. If you try to chase hits, you won't write as well as the people who wrote the hits because you're writing from the wrong perspective. That shouldn't be part of your decision businesswise.

What should be part of your decision businesswise is understanding how the industry works. What gets greenlit is based on some things that you have to keep in mind: Does it attract a director that people have confidence in? Does it attract an actor that financiers feel will be worth spending the money on? Very often, getting the right director gets you the right actors, because they know the actors and certain actors want to work with certain directors. As a matter fact, there are certain actors who will only work with 4 or 5 different directors.

Don't necessarily write with one actor in mind because you don't know if you're going to get that actor. Write the character as a character, as an interesting, compelling, nuanced person. If you do that, there are going to be actors who want to play it. Don't waste your time trying to write for one actor. The chances that you'll get that actor are very small. Stars have material offered to them all the time. They may be busy for 2 years. You may be writing for them based on something they've already done, and they may want to do something different.

Be aware of what's happening in the business so that you're not doing something that's so against current culture that you're defeated before you start. And sometimes that's difficult to ascertain because it's popular culture, and popular culture changes quickly.

Last Words of Advice:

To make it as a professional screenwriter, you have to be determined, stubborn, believe in yourself, keep believing, and most important of all, keep writing (and rewriting)!

These are meant to be guidelines to give you the basics of screenwriting, and help you get your script into sellable shape. There is one last important thing you need to remember as you embark upon your professional screenwriting career:

"Nobody knows anything...... Not one person in the entire motion picture field knows for a certainty what's going to work. Every time out it's a guess and, if you're lucky, an educated one."
> -William Goldman, Adventures in the Screen Trade

Happy writing!

Made in the USA
Monee, IL
18 March 2021